2017-18 STANLEY CUP CHAMPIONS

WASHINGTON CAPITALS

From left: Capitals players Devante Smith-Pelly, Chandler Stephenson, Brett Connolly, Alex Chiasson, Alex Ovechkin and Lars Eller arrive for the first game of the conference finals. (PHOTO BY JONATHAN NEWTON)

The Washington Post

This book is available in quantity at special discounts for your group or organization.
For further information, contact:

Triumph Books LLC
814 North Franklin Street
Chicago, Illinois 60610
Phone: (312) 337-0747
www.triumphbooks.com

Printed in U.S.A.
ISBN: 978-1-62937-557-1

ADDITIONAL CREDITS
Editor: Matthew Rennie. Photo editor: Dudley M. Brooks.
Designer: Brian Gross. Copy editor: Brad Windsor.

Front cover photo by Jonathan Newton.
Back cover photo by Toni L. Sandys.

The Capitals erupted in joyous celebration after winning Game 5 to earn their first Stanley Cup championship. (PHOTO BY JOHN MCDONNELL)

the D
ORLOV
9
SMITH-PELLY
25
74
ORPIK
44
CCM

WASHINGTON

INTRODUCTION

STANLEY CUP CHAMPIONS

Goodbye, ghosts: The past is history

BY THOMAS BOSWELL

A fan crowd-surfs on the sea of red-clad supporters gathered in the streets outside Capital One Arena to watch the Capitals play the Golden Knights in the decisive Game 5. (PHOTO BY MICHAEL ROBINSON CHAVEZ)

The Washington Capitals' march to the 2018 Stanley Cup championship was a combination of exorcism, ghost-busting and curse reversal all rolled into one.

As delirious, and often almost disbelieving, Capitals fans chanted "We want the Cup" inside Capital One Arena, there was something besides a sports title that everyone who cared for the Caps, or for their fans, craved. There was something else that "we" wanted. You could feel it throughout the District at huge downtown watch parties, where thousands stood shoulder to shoulder to cheer as vast images of Caps games were shown on giant screens. And you could sense it in thousands of homes, as well as hundreds of bars and restaurants.

That desire, marinated in a third of a century of sports misery, was for justice, an outcome that reflected simple sports fairness, finally and so ridiculously overdue. Please, can we have a deserved resolution to an old ache? Can we, at last, expunge the Caps' ugly, only partially deserved reputation as gifted inexplicable chokers? And can we replace it with an image of undiluted joy?

Or, if you prefer, a big photo of a gaptoothed, gray-haired, gloriously relieved and proud Alex Ovechkin carrying a Cup that had become an elusive grail. Among the greatest pure goal scorers in hockey history and certainly the best Washington athlete of the past half-century, with his three MVP trophies and seven scoring titles, Ovechkin finally hoisting the Cup ensured that he always will be remembered as a champion.

Beside that image, in memory, in a book or on a wall, put a portrait of star goalie Braden Holtby. Benched on the eve of the playoffs because of a long slump, Holtby was summoned in desperation in the middle of the second game of the first round when it seemed, almost before the postseason had begun, that the Caps would collapse again. Soft-spoken and bearded, Holtby became the quiet eye of the Capitals' swift, creative, hard-hitting, team-centric storm.

Evgeny Kuznetsov and Nicklas Backstrom, two of the most imaginative lightning-strike goal creators who will ever center a pair of lines on the same team, should stand side-by-side. So should versatile T.J. Oshie and valuable defenseman Matt Niskanen, but picture them together getting on Metro to ride D.C.'s subway to home games.

Don't forget a place in the pantheon for defenseman John Carlson, with his huge slap shot on the power play, as well as a symbolic everyman, Devante Smith-Pelly, the fourth-line banger and grinder who scored seven goals all season, then discovered his scoring touch in the playoffs. In his first Caps year, crowds chanted "DSP!"

In the end, after a final victory over the Vegas Golden Knights, Washington had its first championship in any major pro sport in 26 years, and the Caps had their first NHL crown in 44 years of existence.

But perhaps most important, American sports realized that a first-class organization, a consistent winner since the 1982-83 season — and over the past decade the best regular season team in the whole NHL — ultimately would be remembered for its gifts and its best qualities, for its ability to keep hoping and battling, and not solely for 35 years of almost sadistic postseason disappointment.

In a two-month span, through four playoff series, the Caps relived every sad, unlucky or mortifying event that had dogged them since the day the team was born. Name a hockey sin of which the Caps have been accused, and, as they defeated the Columbus Blue Jackets, Pittsburgh Penguins, Tampa Bay Lightning and finally the Golden Knights to win the Cup, they atoned for it.

The Caps faced every charge in the bill of particulars against them and refuted each one. Really, all of them? Yes, all. To understand the size of that task, it helps to have a sense of history and its connection to inexplicable misfortune.

The movie "The Exorcist," set in this very city, came out in 1973. The next year, the hockey team that's always needed an exorcism, the club that made its fans want to screw their heads around backward just for a different view, had its inaugural season: the worst of any team in NHL history, 8-67-5.

The Washington Post sent its youngest sportswriter to interview the least-awful player on that Caps team. The player was defensemen Yvon Labre; the writer was me. From the beginning I have watched the Caps with awe — but the sort of awe usually associated with perplexing and spectacular disasters.

In 1984, the movie "Ghostbusters" appeared. The next season, the Capitals began a third of a century of unprecedented hauntings, including 10 postseasons in which they blew a two-game series lead and 16 in which they were eliminated by lower-seeded teams.

Put another way, in the 32 seasons preceding their glorious Cup, the Caps had missed the playoffs seven times and ended 20 other seasons — twenty! — with a reason to feel rotten due to one or more of the misery-index circumstances mentioned in the previous paragraph. Just five times did they play up to their seeding, getting eliminated with dignity by a better team.

If it seems masochistic to mention all this, remember that, for all of us in our various ways, this amazing Caps Cup has been a gigantic emotional eraser. The memories are still there. But they seem more tolerable now — not in the sense of "it was all worth it" because who could be that Pollyannaish? — but as a kind of badge of allegiance. I covered most of those season-ending losses and still remember the morgue-like rooms and the grief-stricken faces.

Now, with that context, let's recall the gathering disbelief, gradually turning into a frightened joy, that Caps fans felt as series after series, their team dispelled each of its ghouls.

Hockey has never seen anything like this utter reversal of franchise narrative. What gives the Caps' story a glow of parable is that it happened when least expected, when hope had been abandoned by countless fans and optimism had fled from some of the Capitals themselves.

After the Pittsburgh Penguins ripped out their hearts for the second straight year in 2017 and went on to win their second consecutive Stanley Cup, that "0" on the scoreboard beside the Caps' name in Game 7 was a perfect expression of how the NHL culture felt about the franchise. Even worse, some longtime Caps, the core of the team, felt like they might be zeros themselves, though in some way they didn't grasp.

In training camp, feelings were still so raw, self-images so damaged, that fourth-year Coach Barry Trotz told his staff to have a loose rein. "Let them heal," he said. However, 20 games into a dejected start to the season, Trotz called a blunt all-cards-on-the-table meeting in one place he knew he had full attention: 35,000 feet in the air flying back from Colorado after dismal back-to-back loses.

"It was the meeting where you take the big risk — get everything out in the open. After one of those, as a coach, you don't know if they will tune you out," said Trotz, for whom such an ending might have led to his firing. "Or they can all buy in to what you are saying. They were all-in."

And they stayed that way through June.

The series-by-series progression was eerie — and marvelous, because the Caps gained confidence and then a sense of freedom and even fun in their play, with every crisis they met and every old demon they conquered.

In the first round, the Caps lost the first two games at home to lower-seeded Columbus. Instant crisis. Holtby replaced Philipp Grubauer in goal in the middle of the Game 2 loss. Game 3 went two overtimes and was the point at which every happy note that was struck afterward could have gone sour. The Blue Jackets hit four posts in that game, including one late in the third period and another in overtime. Just a one-inch difference, and the Caps would have trailed by three games and their season probably would have ended soon thereafter — unremembered, a dismal continuation of the deflating Ovi Era.

But they won. Then won and won and won, eliminating Columbus in six.

Next up: The Penguins. Sidney Crosby vs. Ovechkin, the latest chapter. Naturally, the Caps lost Game 1 at home. So much for home-ice advantage.

Then the Caps, who aren't supposed to be able to cope with playoff adversity, started losing players. Already absent Andre Burakovsky for the whole series to injury, they lost first-line winger Tom Wilson to a three-game suspension. By Game 6, the invaluable Backstrom was out because of a right index finger that looked like a black-and-blue zucchini.

But then in overtime, with the Capitals leading the series three games to two, Kuznetsov finished a two-on-one rush by taking a pass from Ovechkin and shooting the puck between Matt Murray's knees for the series clincher. Cross off: Crosby Curse, Pens Hex, blown home-ice edge and can't cope with adversity.

The toughest test may have been in the Eastern Conference finals against a Lightning team that led the NHL in scoring. The Caps immediately laid an insidious trap — for themselves. By playing brilliantly and winning the first two games on the road, the Caps were suddenly big favorites again, in a position where 21 of 22 previous teams had advanced. That's wonderful — until you lose the next three games.

Suddenly, even though the Caps' entire season might have been considered an overachieving success, the team was once again in the position to end its year with egg on its face. Once more, Washington would be reminded that its team, including seven key players who had been together for seven seasons at least, would never reach the Stanley Cup finals as a group.

The Caps, the team that never supposedly rises to the occasion against tough competition for high stakes, not only won the last two games but dominated the Lightning, outscoring Tampa Bay by a combined 7-0 as Holtby, who hadn't had a shutout all season, got a pair of them.

The Stanley Cup finals began much as the Caps' only previous appearance had 20 years ago — with an opening-game loss on the road. Team history says that a potentially cheerful season must end by getting swept. That's what the Red Wings did to the Caps in 1998, and what the Bruins did in the conference finals in 1990, and what the Lightning did in 2011, when the Caps had rolled past the Rangers and seemed headed for a deep playoff run.

Instead, finally, the last of the curses was "swept" away. The Caps, the team that so often seemed to get snuffed by the "hot goalie," suddenly had its own in Holtby. Some franchises have so many "signature moments," so many indelible instants that remain framed in our minds and even on our walls, that you can't keep them straight.

Now, the Caps have The Save, as Holtby, defending a 3-2 lead at the end of Game 2, pulled off a tougher robbery than looting the vault at Caesars, sprawling to stop a point-blank shot from Vegas's Alex Tuch.

Perhaps that's when Washington finally allowed itself to believe that optimism in sports is not a disease, that rooting for the Capitals can be as great a delight as it has been a burden, and that this idea of investing many years in chasing, and capturing, a championship is an experience that a team and an entire city can share and remember. For as long as they want.

No ghosts, demons or curses allowed.

BACKSTROM
19

STANLEY CUP FINALS

CAPITALS 4, KNIGHTS 1

All champs

BY RICK MAESE

Alex Ovechkin passed the Stanley Cup to Nicklas Backstrom, who has passed countless pucks to him during their decade together. (PHOTO BY TONI L. SANDYS)

When time expired and the helmets and sticks were tossed into the air, the Washington Capitals poured onto the ice, and a celebration decades in the making ensued. The players hugged each other in joy and shook each other in disbelief.

Team captain Alex Ovechkin was on the edge of the scrum, bouncing and screaming, trying to make sure his voice could be heard from Las Vegas to Washington to Moscow.

As the trophy made its way onto the ice, some 2,400 miles away, a sea of red — jubilant Capitals fans who filled the streets in downtown Washington — erupted, too. The win was a season in the making for many on the ice and a lifetime in the making for so many fans back home. The Stanley Cup, the most storied trophy in sports, is coming to Washington, courtesy of a pair of Russian scoring machines, a journeyman-turned-hero, an unflappable goaltender and a supporting cast that confronted a season's worth of challenges with careers' worth of determination.

The Capitals topped the final foe, the Vegas Golden Knights, 4-3, in exciting fashion Thursday night in Game 5 of the Stanley Cup finals. The comeback victory gave the Capitals a four-games-to-one series victory and secured the first NHL championship in the franchise's 44-year history — and the city's first title in any of the four major American sports in more than a quarter-century.

"I can't explain what I feel," Ovechkin said when it was over. "It's unbelievable."

The finale was tense from start to finish: the hard hits in the opening period, the explosion of scoring in the second and the winning goal off the stick of center Lars Eller in the third. It amounted to three periods of racing hearts and bated breath, electrifying a region of sports fans well-versed in disappointment but largely unaccustomed to the sensation that suddenly swept over them late Thursday night.

After Vegas built a 3-2 lead in the second period, Washington had to claw its way back and did so thanks to one of the most unlikely stars of these playoffs. Forward Devante Smith-Pelly scored a total of seven goals in the regular season. His tying goal at the 9:52 mark in the third period was his seventh of the postseason, his third of the finals.

Barely two minutes later, the Capitals struck again. Vegas goaltender Marc-Andre Fleury blocked Brett Connolly's shot but didn't secure the puck. Eller was positioned perfectly on the edge of the crease, scooping the puck from behind Fleury and into the net.

The pair of quick scores lit a fire under the raucous contingent of red-clad fans who made the trek west for the game — not to mention the thousands who had turned much of the Washington region into a giant outdoor party. Many of them had dreamed of this moment for years yet were still wholly unprepared for it.

Fans hugged strangers. Strangers high-fived police officers. Cab drivers stopped their cars to take pictures. Everyone seemed to pause in the middle of the street just to scream. The scene was mayhem, the soundtrack of horns everywhere, honking in rhythm.

Near Capital One Arena in Northwest, Seventh Street was packed, overflowing. People sprinted down H Street, screaming, cursing. Cars everywhere honked the "Let's Go Caps" rhythm. Fans chanted "C-A-P-S" and screamed. Traffic nearby didn't move, and the honks provided a chorus to a celebration that grew as more and more people ran into the mayhem.

"Congratulations," they screamed to strangers, voices cracking.

"My goal was always to build a team as good as the fan base," Capitals owner Ted Leonsis said. "I think we have the best fans in the world, and now we have the best hockey team in the world."

This was, in fact, among the most unlikely Capitals teams to make a deep run. Some analysts speculated after last season's early playoff exit that it was time for the Capitals to move on from Ovechkin. The team parted ways with a handful of key players last offseason and opted against an extension for Coach Barry Trotz, whose contract expires July 1.

The Capitals had a losing record one month into the season, and their flashes of brilliance were often matched by inexplicable lapses. The Capitals didn't assume first place in the Metropolitan Division to stay until March 10 and finished the regular season tied for the conference's third-best record.

"Throughout the whole year, not a lot was expected out of us," forward T.J. Oshie said. "Maybe on paper we weren't as elite as teams past. But man, did we ever come together."

Still, they looked little like the team that would start to coalesce several weeks later, losing their first two games of the playoffs against the Columbus Blue Jackets, sending fans on a familiar ride of disappointment. But Trotz switched goaltenders, replacing Philipp Grubauer with Braden Holtby, and the Capitals started getting the kinds of bounces that once eluded them. They clawed their way back to oust the Blue Jackets, and their reward was a second-round matchup against the Pittsburgh Penguins, a nemesis that had bested the Capitals in their previous seven postseason meetings, including each of the past two years.

But Ovechkin, Evgeny Kuznetsov and the Capitals kept scoring, Holtby kept shining in net, and Washington bound over the second-round hurdle that had been so insurmountable. In the conference finals, they'd need all seven games to top Tampa Bay and punch a ticket to the Stanley Cup finals. Vegas was an expansion franchise that surprised throughout the regular season and playoffs, including in Thursday's whirlwind second period in which the Golden Knights scored three times. But the Capitals showed resilience, seasoned by years of hope and disappointment and star players who will be treated like heroes in D.C. for a long time.

"To me, they changed all the narratives," Trotz said, "checked off every box. ... It was probably fitting we were down in this game and had to come back."

After the game was finished and the Capitals had completed the comeback, the Stanley Cup was carried onto the ice. NHL Commissioner Gary Berman called up Ovechkin first.

Overcome with emotions, the 32-year-old captain lifted the trophy over his head, planted a kiss on it and took it for spin down the ice, showing off the sport's biggest prize for the rest of the world. He passed it off to Nicklas Backstrom, who gave it to Brooks Orpik. And then Oshie and Jay Beagle and Holtby. It was passed from player to player, champion to champion.

Every one of them had been reminded over and over how Washington teams disappoint, how the Capitals, especially, break hearts. They shrugged off history. They made history. They're bringing the Stanley Cup to Washington, a city that's waited more than a quarter-century to celebrate a champion.

Dan Steinberg contributed from Washington.

GAME 1

KNIGHTS 6, CAPITALS 4

Welcome to the Wild West

By Isabelle Khurshudyan

Alex Ovechkin walked into the locker room, a beanie on his head and a Washington Capitals sweatshirt over his chest. He was struggling to catch his breath, so much so that a team staffer offered to grab him a bottle of water. He was exhausted after a high-paced game that was exactly what the opponent wanted.

"A little nervous overall," Ovechkin admitted.

It was the first game of a first Stanley Cup finals for the bulk of both the Vegas and Washington rosters — and the action was riveting but unfortunate for the Capitals. They lost, 6-4, keeping pace with the speedy Golden Knights until they couldn't, playing a game that wasn't well-suited to Washington's tight-checking identity.

"They were a little quicker than us," Capitals forward Brett Connolly said. "You don't want to be trading chances with any team. There's two good teams. We can score, too. Ten goals tonight. But no team wants to be trading chances back and forth because then it's up in the air as to who is going to score those goals."

Game 1 of the Stanley Cup finals is often a feeling-out process for both teams, though the club that wins it is crowned champion roughly 78 percent of the time. For all the plays leading up to the fateful one, for all the frenetic action at both ends of the rink, the game-winner came down to two fourth lines on the ice. Devante Smith-Pelly failed to clear the puck out of the Washington end, and Golden Knights defenseman Shea Theodore then set up Tomas Nosek's backdoor strike with 10:16 to play.

It was the ninth goal — good news for those who bet the over — in a game that felt as improbable as the two teams playing it. On one bench were the Capitals, who waited a long 20 years to get back to this stage, making their first trip to the finals with the superstar core of Ovechkin and Nicklas Backstrom. On the other bench were the Golden Knights, who waited all of one year, an expansion franchise in its inaugural season that somehow shunned conventional wisdom by making a deep playoff run so quickly.

"I don't think [anybody] believes in us and nobody believes in Vegas, and we're right now in the Stanley Cup finals and we fight for a Cup," Ovechkin said Sunday.

The back-and-forth action was fit for a show on the Las Vegas Strip. With the teams tied at three goals apiece entering the third period, Washington's Tom Wilson jammed a puck through Golden Knights goaltender Marc-Andre Fleury, who then kicked it into his own net just 1:10 into the frame.

Less than two minutes later, physical fourth-line forward Ryan Reaves punched a puck in from point-blank range to again tie the game for Vegas. Reaves was on the ice again seven minutes later, when Nosek scored the game-winner. Nosek then added the empty-net insurance in the final seconds.

"I think that was probably exciting for the fans but not exactly a clean hockey game for either side," Capitals goaltender Braden Holtby said.

Defenseman Matt Niskanen said, "A lot of energy and a little bit of rust can lead to that kind of play." The Capitals also had to adjust to uncomfortable ice conditions — the puck bounced on a sheet that had to withstand desert heat outside the arena.

"The ice isn't great, or they didn't freeze the pucks or something," Niskanen said. "Not ideal conditions, but they're playing with it, too."

The Capitals were prepared for a strong start from the Golden Knights, who were feeding off the energy of their raucous crowd and then vice versa. Vegas took an early lead when defenseman Colin Miller scored a power-play goal 7:15 into the game with a blast from the left point, his shot winding through two layers of screens. The Golden Knights entered Monday's game with a 10-1 record in the postseason when scoring first.

But Washington seemed to push past its nerves and settle into the charged atmosphere. Earlier in the season, Ovechkin said the Golden Knights' T-Mobile Arena is "like you're in a nightclub. It's like a party. Everybody dancing over there. It's like, 'Holy Jesus, are we in a hockey game, or is this like a pool party out there?'"

Showgirls lined the glass by the Capitals' end of the rink during warmups. Two rows of Elvis impersonators — and one person in a gorilla suit — sat along the glass next to Washington's bench. A long and elaborate pregame ceremony pushed back the drop of the puck. Famous ring announcer Michael Buffer read the starting lineup on the ice just as he would before a championship bout. Ovechkin skated in circles, antsy and anxious for the game to start.

The Capitals responded 14:41 into the game, when Connolly redirected Michal Kempny's point shot through his legs and past Fleury, who entered the game with an impressive .947 save percentage during these playoffs. Less than a minute later, forward T.J. Oshie lost the puck on a wraparound attempt, but Backstrom, playing with an injured right index finger, punched it past Fleury's extended left pad.

The Golden Knights took the lead with a pair of goals, and then the Caps did the same. But two fourth-line goals late in the third period put Vegas up for good, the house winning once more.

"They're a fast team, and we know that," Backstrom said. "They're going to put some pressure on us. But overall, I thought we were a little sloppy with the puck. We didn't make the plays that we usually do. I think we can play a little quicker, more north. That's what we've got to do."

MAY 28 AT VEGAS

Capitals	**2**	**1**	**1**	**4**
Golden Knights	**2**	**1**	**3**	**6**

FIRST PERIOD

Scoring: 1, Vegas, Miller 3 (Haula), 7:15 (pp). 2, Washington, Connolly 5 (Burakovsky, Kempny), 14:41. 3, Washington, Backstrom 5 (Oshie, Vrana), 15:23. 4, Vegas, Karlsson 7 (Smith, Engelland), 18:19.

SECOND PERIOD

Scoring: 5, Vegas, Smith 3 (Marchessault, Engelland), 3:21. 6, Washington, Carlson 4 (Backstrom, Oshie), 8:29.

THIRD PERIOD

Scoring: 7, Washington, Wilson 4 (Kuznetsov, Ovechkin), 1:10. 8, Vegas, Reaves 2, 2:41. 9, Vegas, Nosek 2 (Theodore), 9:44.
10, Vegas, Nosek 3 (Perron), 19:57.

SHOTS ON GOAL

Washington	10	8	10	28
Vegas	11	14	9	34

Power-play opportunities:
Washington 0 of 1; Vegas 1 of 1.

Goalies: Washington, Holtby 12-7 (33 shots-28 saves). Vegas, Fleury 13-3 (28-24).

A long pregame ceremony delayed the start of the series opener, and then the teams put on a high-scoring show. (PHOTO BY TONI L. SANDYS)

89
TUCH

GAME 2

CAPITALS 3, KNIGHTS 2

Winning hand: Caps hang on to even series

By Isabelle Khurshudyan

Braden Holtby made a game-saving stop on a point-blank shot by Vegas right wing Alex Tuch late in the third period. (PHOTO BY TONI L. SANDYS)

MAY 30 AT VEGAS

Capitals	**1**	**2**	**0**	**3**
Golden Knights	**1**	**1**	**0**	**2**

FIRST PERIOD

Scoring: 1, Vegas, Neal 5 (Sbisa, Miller), 7:58. 2, Washington, Eller 6 (Burakovsky, Kempny), 17:27.

SECOND PERIOD

Scoring: 3, Washington, Ovechkin 13 (Backstrom, Eller), 5:38 (pp). 4, Washington, Orpik 1 (Burakovsky, Eller), 9:41. 5, Vegas, Theodore 3 (Smith, Karlsson), 17:47 (pp).

THIRD PERIOD

Scoring: None.

SHOTS ON GOAL

Washington	11	9	6	26
Vegas	10	14	15	39

Power-play opportunities:
Washington 1 of 2; Vegas 1 of 5.

Goalies: Washington, Holtby 13-7 (39 shots-37 saves). Vegas, Fleury 13-4 (26-23).

Evgeny Kuznetsov was grimacing, clearly in pain as he skated off the ice. He didn't pause as he walked straight down the tunnel leading to the Washington Capitals' locker room, and the team's dream playoff run was suddenly looking like a nightmare without its top scorer.

But less than three minutes later, there was center Lars Eller smiling and laughing in disbelief. "What a pass," he said to Capitals defenseman Michal Kempny as the two hugged. They had connected for a tally that tied the game and seemed to revive Washington as the team reeled off three unanswered goals in a 3-2 win in Game 2 of the Stanley Cup finals against the Vegas Golden Knights. Eller played a part in all three, assisting on Alex Ovechkin's and Brooks Orpik's goals in the second period.

Kuznetsov didn't return to the game, and it's unclear how long Washington will be without its No. 1 center. But on Wednesday night, the Capitals persevered in large part because of Eller's effort against the Golden Knights, tying the series at a game apiece with the next two games in Washington. This was the first Stanley Cup finals game win in franchise history.

"You lose one of our top players ... your bench sort of rallies around it," Capitals Coach Barry Trotz said. "Obviously, a guy like Lars Eller, when all of a sudden Kuzy's not back, Lars has to step into that role. He just stepped up."

The most unlikely of game-winning goals came 9:41 into the second period, from a stay-at-home defenseman who hadn't scored in more than two years. Eller carried the puck into the offensive zone before passing it to Orpik in the left faceoff circle. Orpik's point shot clipped forward Alex Tuch's elbow, taking an unpredictable bounce in front of Vegas goaltender Marc-Andre Fleury to get past him and lift Washington to a 3-1 lead. Orpik's last goal was in February 2016.

"I haven't yelled that loud for someone to score a goal since [Alex Ovechkin] scored one of his milestones," forward T.J. Oshie said.

Golden Knights defenseman Shea Theodore made it a one-goal game with his power-play goal later in the second period, and then Capitals goaltender Braden Holtby saved the game late in the third with arguably the best save of the postseason, an outstretched stick denying Tuch's point-blank shot in the final two minutes of the game. Holtby finished with 37 saves, none more important or stunning than that one.

"I honestly thought for a second there, when it bounced right out to them, I was like, 'Oh, no,'" center Nicklas Backstrom said. "But then I was like, 'Oh, yes.'"

Said Holtby: "I was just trying to get something there, trying to see where I thought someone would shoot that, and luckily it hit me."

Teams struggle to survive the first 10 minutes at T-Mobile Arena, as the Golden Knights have made a habit out of scoring early. Less than eight minutes into the game, Vegas defenseman Luca Sbisa lofted a pass through the neutral zone, and Washington's Dmitry Orlov attempted to bat down the high puck near the blue line but missed. Golden Knights forward James Neal got an open chance as a result, beating Holtby from the left faceoff circle. Through nine home playoff games, Vegas has scored the first goal in the first 10 minutes six times, and the team fell to 11-2 in the postseason when scoring first.

The game went from bad to worse for the Capitals. With 5:21 left in the first period, Golden Knights defenseman Brayden McNabb crunched Kuznetsov against the glass, and Kuznetsov skated off the ice in distress, clutching his left arm or wrist. He retreated to the locker room and didn't play the rest of the game because of an undisclosed "upper-body" injury. Trotz didn't have an update immediately after the game, but he considered McNabb's hit "questionable."

Depending on the severity of the injury, the loss could be devastating for the Capitals. Kuznetsov has been Washington's leading scorer during the playoffs with 11 goals and 14 assists through 21 games.

With Kuznetsov out, Nicklas Backstrom centered the top trio with Ovechkin and Tom Wilson while Eller's role was elevated to a second line with wingers Oshie and Jakub Vrana. During a stretch of four-on-four play less than three minutes after

Alex Ovechkin banged on the glass after scoring in the second period of Game 2. (PHOTO BY TONI L. SANDYS)

Kuznetsov got hurt, winger Andre Burakovsky won a battle along the boards, falling down as he flung the puck to Kempny on the left side. With Fleury turned to the left, Kempny passed the puck across the slot to Eller in the right circle, and Eller one-timed the puck into a half-open net to tie the game.

It was redemption for the 29-year-old Dane, who has played well this postseason. In the final minute of Game 1, Eller had a chance to tie the game with a tap-in at the goal mouth, but he wasn't able to get his stick on the puck after he was arguably slashed by McNabb on the play. "There's tough breaks during a series and during a season," Eller said Tuesday. "Give me 100 of those, I'll put 99 in."

Before Tuesday's practice, Eller was tabbed to skate the hot lap, a trip around the ice that has become a road tradition for the Capitals during these playoffs. He didn't disclose why he was selected, but perhaps his teammates sensed he would play an important role for them in Wednesday's Game 2. He finished third among Capitals forwards in ice time, behind just Backstrom and Oshie. "Yeah, he's a guy who is kind of our secret weapon," Ovechkin said. "It's hard to play [against him] when he's on top of his game and when he feels the puck, when he creates the moment for us. He was pretty big for us."

Taking Kuznetsov's place on the top power-play unit, Eller then helped Washington take the lead. Tuch was called for cross-checking in the offensive zone, and the Capitals capitalized with a tic-tac-toe sequence with Eller recording the primary assist on Ovechkin's power-play snap-shot strike. Eller capped a three-point performance with his helper on Orpik's improbable goal, which gave Washington a 3-1 lead midway through the second period.

"He just played outstanding," Oshie said. "It seems like he's one of those guys who has a knack for the stage, for the extra responsibilities, and he does a great job with it."

NBA
WORLD
CHAMPIONS
1977-78
capitals
hulu

GAME 3

CAPITALS 3, KNIGHTS 1

On home ice, stars give Caps series lead

By Isabelle Khurshudyan

Fans waved glowing sticks before the Capitals' first home game in the Stanley Cup finals since 1998. (PHOTO BY RICKY CARIOTI)

JUNE 2 AT WASHINGTON

Golden Knights	**0**	**0**	**1**	**1**
Capitals	**0**	**2**	**1**	**3**

FIRST PERIOD

Scoring: None.

SECOND PERIOD

Scoring: 1, Washington, Ovechkin 14 (Kuznetsov, Carlson), 1:10. 2, Washington, Kuznetsov 12 (Beagle, Oshie), 12:50.

THIRD PERIOD

Scoring: 3, Vegas, Nosek 4 (Bellemare), 3:29. 4, Washington, Smith-Pelly 5 (Beagle), 13:53.

SHOTS ON GOAL

Vegas	5	8	9	22
Washington	7	14	5	26

Power-play opportunities:
Vegas 0 for 2; Washington 0 for 4.

Goalies: Vegas, Fleury 13-5 (26 shots-23 saves). Washington, Holtby 14-7 (22-21).

Evgeny Kuznetsov flapped his wings, Alex Ovechkin stood on the bench and roared with both arms raised as Lars Eller happily rubbed the captain's stomach, and Capital One Arena answered his roar with an even louder one. The Stanley Cup finals had arrived in Washington, and the Capitals rose to the moment.

Washington won Game 3 of the best-of-seven series, 3-1, on Saturday night for a two-games-to-one lead over the Vegas Golden Knights. The Capitals' stars carried them, from Ovechkin scoring the first goal to Kuznetsov building on the lead to goaltender Braden Holtby pitching a shutout through 40 minutes and turning away 21 of 22 shots for the game. Washington played its game perfectly, suffocating the Golden Knights and holding them to just 13 shots through two periods.

The organization's first Stanley Cup finals home win was sealed when Jay Beagle set up Devante Smith-Pelly, who beat Vegas goaltender Marc-Andre Fleury from point-blank range at 13:53 of the third period to make it 3-1. A wave of red leaped to its feet, "Let's go Caps" chants following shortly after. Washington's two-goal lead was restored, and the Golden Knights' push fell short. It was a moment of redemption for Smith-Pelly, who had taken two penalties earlier in the game.

"It's nuts right now, and it's great to see," defenseman John Carlson said. "They deserve us to get there, and we've got a long ways to go, but you always have to take it in and have fun with it."

It had been 20 years since Washington hosted a Stanley Cup finals game, and the lower bowl of Capital One Arena was largely full as warmups began. More than 14,000 fans had shown up to watch Games 1 and 2 here, even though the Capitals were playing in Las Vegas. Sting and Shaggy performed a concert on the Smithsonian National Portrait Gallery steps before the game, and "Wheel of Fortune" host Pat Sajak announced the starting lineups. After a drawn-out buildup, foam red glowing sticks waved wildly in anticipation of puck drop.

"I've never seen the fans like this," forward T.J. Oshie said before the game. "They're always good, but I've never seen them like this."

Home ice had been bittersweet for Washington this postseason. The Capitals entered Saturday night with a 4-5 record in Chinatown during these playoffs, but their last game here had been positive: a Game 6 shutout of the Tampa Bay Lightning in the Eastern Conference finals. It offered Washington a formula for success against the Golden Knights, who had lost just two games on the road this postseason.

"The further the playoff has gone, we are playing smarter, not taking too many risks," center Nicklas Backstrom said. "I feel like that's the way you have to play. You have to play good defensively, and that's what we're doing right now."

The Capitals got good news before the game: Kuznetsov was back in the lineup after a scare in Game 2. He suffered an undisclosed "upper-body" injury Wednesday when Vegas defenseman Brayden McNabb crunched him against the glass in the first period, forcing Washington's top center and leading scorer to miss the rest of the game.

Kuznetsov looked good on his first shift Saturday when, on a two-on-one, his saucer pass skipped over McNabb and went right to Ovechkin's stick. But Fleury made the highlight-reel save on the first shot of the game. Ovechkin had eight shot attempts in the first period alone.

"I feel like Ovi always has about 10 shots on goal halfway through the game, or he has the attempts at least," Eller said. "He was pumped up. Everybody was pumped up today."

The Capitals had another close call when forward Chandler Stephenson beat Fleury, sniping the puck past him. But the goal was immediately waved off; Smith-Pelly had made contact with Fleury in the crease, his backside catching the goaltender's head. In a significant swing, Smith-Pelly went to the box for goaltender interference, and the Golden Knights got a power play.

After taking two penalties, Devante Smith-Pelly earned redemption with a third-period goal. (PHOTO BY RICKY CARIOTI)

But the Capitals withstood that push, neither team breaking through in the first period. Then Ovechkin and Kuznetsov were rewarded coming out of intermission. Barely a minute into the period, Washington took several whacks at a puck bouncing in front of Fleury. Ovechkin punched in a rebound on the fifth try, lifting Washington to a one-goal lead at 1:10.

Then, 12:50 into the period, after an extended shift by the Golden Knights, Beagle finally cleared the puck to create a two-on-one with Kuznetsov. Kuznetsov held on to the puck and then calmly shot it past Fleury. There had been some concern that he had injured his wrist on the collision with McNabb in the previous game, but that shot assured he was feeling just fine.

"It's emotional stuff," Kuznetsov said. "Like Michael Jordan, when he play his best game — he got hurt."

Kuznetsov kicked up a leg and stretched out his arms as he mimicked a bird, a celebration that's a favorite with his young daughter. On the bench, Ovechkin stood, raised both arms and screamed as teammates hugged him. The Stanley Cup was on display in Section 204 of Capital One Arena before the game, and now the Capitals are two wins from claiming it as their own for the first time.

"It's obviously fun for us to see the city like this and bring that kind of energy and enjoyment," Holtby said. "The fans have been phenomenal. But in saying that, our group as professionals, you get more out of making that sacrifice so everyone can enjoy it. So we're just putting our head down, focusing on Game 4 to keep working toward that big goal."

EASTON
NEAL
18
BAUER

GAME 4

CAPITALS 6, KNIGHTS 2

Lopsided win puts Caps on the cusp

By Isabelle Khurshudyan

Vegas left wing James Neal lost his stick after slashing Tom Wilson, and Washington scored on the ensuing power play to take a 4-0 lead. (PHOTO BY JOHN MCDONNELL)

JUNE 4 AT WASHINGTON

Golden Knights	**0**	**0**	**2**	**2**
Capitals	**3**	**1**	**2**	**6**

FIRST PERIOD

Scoring: 1, Washington, Oshie 8 (Kuznetsov, Backstrom), 9:54 (pp). 2, Washington, Wilson 5 (Kuznetsov), 16:26. 3, Washington, Smith-Pelly 6 (Ovechkin, Niskanen), 19:39.

SECOND PERIOD

Scoring: 4, Washington, Carlson 5 (Kuznetsov, Oshie), 15:23 (pp).

THIRD PERIOD

Scoring: 5, Vegas, Neal 6 (Miller, Haula), 5:43. 6, Vegas, Smith 4 (Sbisa, Marchessault), 12:26. 7, Washington, Kempny 2 (Oshie, Backstrom), 13:39. 8, Washington, Connolly 6 (Kuznetsov, Backstrom), 18:51 (pp).

SHOTS ON GOAL

Vegas	11	11	8	30
Washington	10	5	8	23

Power-play opportunities:
Vegas 0 of 4; Washington 3 of 5.

Goalies: Vegas, Fleury 13-5 (23 shots-17 saves). Washington, Holtby 14-7 (30-28).

Washington Capitals center Evgeny Kuznetsov plopped down in his dressing room stall Saturday and smirked at the crowd of reporters around him. After an injury scare that caused him to miss most of Game 2 of the Stanley Cup finals, Kuznetsov was seemingly no worse for wear — and luckily so.

"I think I'm born lucky," Kuznetsov said with shrug and a smile.

Two nights later, against a team from Las Vegas of all places, all of Capital One Arena looked lucky Monday night when the Capitals pulled within one win of their first Stanley Cup championship with a 6-2 victory over the Golden Knights in Game 4. Washington took a three-games-to-one series lead as Vegas hit three posts, perhaps retribution for all the bad bounces that have previously haunted the franchise. A lot has differentiated this Capitals team from past renditions, but perhaps nothing more so than fortune in a game where a frozen disk of vulcanized rubber can rattle around in so many directions.

But then Washington capitalized on the breaks and poured it on — it was both lucky and good. Thanks to three early primary assists from Kuznetsov, who finished with four points total and is just the fifth player since 1997 to record more than 30 points in a single postseason, the Capitals reeled off the first four goals to take control of the game and this finals series. With the game well in hand with less than four minutes left, fans fearlessly chanted, "We want the Cup."

"That is what you play for, so I think you use it for emotion," forward Tom Wilson said. "You use it to drive you forward. That's it. You don't think too far ahead, but that is what you are playing for and it is there the whole playoffs."

Coach Barry Trotz has often spoke of the "hockey gods," and they seemed to be smiling on his team from the start. Vegas forward Erik Haula tipped a shot just 1:07 into the first period, but the puck caromed off the post. That lucky break didn't compare to the one Washington got 4:31 into the game, when James Neal had a wide-open net to shoot into with Capitals goaltender Braden Holtby out of position during a Golden Knights power play. Neal inexplicably hit the post, squandering an opportunity to lift Vegas to an early lead.

"To be honest, I thought it was in from my angle, and somehow it didn't go in," Holtby said. "I thought we worked for our breaks tonight, though. ... We want to do everything in our power so we don't need breaks to win. We can just focus on our game, do the little things right and keep pushing forward."

To that point, the Golden Knights had pressured the Capitals with some of their best chances in the past three games. But Washington took advantage of its fortune. Vegas defenseman Colin Miller stuck a leg out to blatantly trip center Lars Eller 9:22 into the game, and 32 seconds into the subsequent power play, Capitals winger T.J. Oshie scored on a rebound of Kuznetsov's shot. Oshie went on to add two assists.

Though play continued to be fairly even throughout the first period, Washington made the scoreboard lopsided. Kuznetsov set up a Wilson wrister that extended the Capitals' lead to two through 16:26. Kuznetsov has points in 13 of his past 14 playoff games — he didn't record a point in Game 2, when he missed the final two periods with an "upper-body" injury — and he is the postseason's leading scorer with 12 goals and 19 assists, a leading candidate to win the Conn Smythe Trophy as the most valuable player of the playoffs.

Kuznetsov was on the ice for the Capitals' third goal, too. Washington defenseman Matt Niskanen's shot was blocked by Jonathan Marchessault in front of the net, but the puck bounced over to forward Devante Smith-Pelly, who punched it past goaltender Marc-Andre Fleury. Fleury had a .947 save percentage entering this series, but the Capitals have now scored 16 goals on him through four games.

Two Golden Knights fans were surrounded by celebrating Caps faithful after Washington's final goal. (PHOTO BY JOHN MCDONNELL)

"It could have been a different hockey game if they scored on their power play, so we got a little lucky there," center Nicklas Backstrom said. "Yeah, I don't know, maybe it shouldn't have been a 3-0 lead after the first, but, you know, we will take it. We are not going to feel sorry for them."

It was a a display of everything that has carried Washington. The power play has been dangerous, and the Capitals' stars have found ways to produce at even strength. Washington has also gotten secondary scoring, goals from unheralded players such as Smith-Pelly, who had just seven in the regular season and now has six through 23 playoff games.

Less than nine minutes into the second period, the Golden Knights hit a third post when Brayden McNabb's wrist shot pinged away from Holtby. But when shots got through, Holtby was sharp, recording 22 saves through two periods and 28 overall. In a change from past Washington playoff runs, the Capitals have the hot goaltender; Holtby has allowed just five goals on 91 shots in three straight wins.

After Vegas's power play had folded on its first three tries, Neal was called for slashing 14:45 into the second period. With defenseman John Carlson in Alex Ovechkin's usual sweet spot in the left faceoff circle, Oshie got tangled up with Vegas's Cody Eakin, clearing a lane for Kuznetsov to set up Carlson's one-timer. With the Capitals up by four goals, Carlson screamed as teammates circled around him. Kuznetsov was the fifth player there, his teammates taking turns patting him on the helmet.

Maybe you have to be good to be lucky.

CHAMPS
CHAMPS
CCM
A
C
adidas
HOLTBY
70
SMITH-PELLY
25

GAME 5

CAPITALS 4, KNIGHTS 3

Caps hoist the Cup as 44-year wait ends

By Isabelle Khurshudyan

Capitals owner Ted Leonsis, raising the Stanley Cup for the first time, said, "Now we have the best hockey team in the world." (PHOTO BY JOHN MCDONNELL)

JUNE 7 AT VEGAS

Capitals	**0**	**2**	**2**	**4**
Golden Knights	**0**	**3**	**0**	**3**

FIRST PERIOD
Scoring: None.

SECOND PERIOD
Scoring: 1, Washington, Vrana 3 (Kuznetsov, Wilson), 6:24. 2, Vegas, Schmidt 3 (Marchessault, Smith), 9:40. 3, Washington, Ovechkin 15 (Backstrom, Carlson), 10:14 (pp). 4, Vegas, Perron 1 (Miller, Tatar), 12:56. 5, Vegas, Smith 5 (Tuch, Theodore), 19:31 (pp).

THIRD PERIOD
Scoring: 6, Washington, Smith-Pelly 7 (Orpik), 9:52. 7, Washington, Eller 7 (Burakovsky, Connolly), 12:23.

SHOTS ON GOAL

Washington	9	11	13	33
Vegas	7	13	11	31

Power-play opportunities:
Washington 1 of 4; Vegas 1 of 2.

Goalies: Washington, Holtby 15-7 (31 shots-28 saves). Vegas, Fleury 13-6 (33-29).

Alex Ovechkin tossed off his helmet and gloves early, with his Washington Capitals less than a second away from winning the Stanley Cup. One last faceoff remained. The puck dropped, the clock stopped for good, and Ovechkin looked skyward — lifting his arms, running his fingers through his gray hair, perhaps disbelieving that a moment he seemed destined for had finally arrived 13 seasons into his NHL career.

The fans in the streets of Washington and those in T-Mobile Arena did the same. They had been patient, too, waiting 44 years for the Capitals to be crowned Stanley Cup champions after they defeated the Vegas Golden Knights in five games with Thursday's 4-3 win. Ovechkin skated to the glass and blew kisses to the crowd.

Then Ovechkin turned to each of his teammates, screaming as he was asked by NHL Commissioner Gary Bettman to lift the Stanley Cup for the first time. He screamed again when he touched it. He kept screaming when he raised it overhead.

The Capitals had been stained with the loser label since 1974-75, when the expansion team won just eight games, still the NHL's worst campaign. Ovechkin's arrival in 2004, drafted first overall, eventually brought more regular season success, and with a young superstar core of him and center Nicklas Backstrom, a first championship felt inevitable. Ovechkin has admitted that he treated it as such at times, perhaps taking for granted how hard it can be to win.

That lesson was learned with repeated playoff disappointments: Nine trips to the postseason ended short of the conference finals. Ovechkin's leadership and commitment were questioned. It was fair to question whether Washington's talented foundation was damaged — and whether this year was its last chance to prove it deserved to stay together.

It was fitting that the Capitals won their first Stanley Cup with Backstrom setting up an Ovechkin power-play goal. They have complemented each other for a decade, the flashy goal scorer in Ovechkin (named the Conn Smythe winner as playoff MVP) and the subtle and skilled setup man in Backstrom. They played on separate lines this postseason after years side by side, but they acknowledged each other at every step of this journey. Backstrom had to miss Washington's clinching Game 6 win against Pittsburgh in the second round because of a right hand injury, but after the Capitals got past the Penguins for their first trip to the Eastern Conference finals in 20 years, Ovechkin hugged Backstrom in the dressing room. They shared another embrace on the ice when Washington won Game 7 against Tampa Bay in the conference finals.

On Thursday night, after Ovechkin hoisted and kissed the Stanley Cup, he passed it to Backstrom, an acknowledgment of their long partnership.

This season started with the same Stanley Cup dreams, but perhaps the Capitals were the only ones who considered them realistic.

"We're not going to be suck this year," Ovechkin said on the first day of training camp. Washington couldn't get past the second round with rosters that won the Presidents' Trophy for the league's best regular season title in back-to-back seasons, and after salary cap constraints coupled with the expansion draft caused significant roster turnover, there was little optimism that this would be the Capitals' year.

Veterans were replaced with rookies and fringe NHLers. Winger Jakub Vrana, the team's 2014 first-round pick, was counted on to produce offensively in his first full season. He endured goal droughts that lasted months, and he was a healthy scratch at the start of the playoffs. But on Thursday night, he scored the first goal of the game on a breakaway. Veteran Capitals have said the infusion of youth was a big reason for the team's success; the youngsters didn't know playoff heartbreak, playing without the burden of the organization's tortured history.

The same could be said for the team's unheralded free agent additions. At 25, Devante Smith-Pelly had his contract bought out by the New Jersey Devils, and he signed with Washington for the league minimum. It wasn't clear whether he would even make the team out of training camp, but after Smith-Pelly scored seven goals during the regular season, he matched that total in the playoffs. His seventh goal and third

in as many games came with 10:08 left in regulation Thursday, tying the score at 3.

Consider that this improbable run probably wouldn't have lasted past the team's first-round series had a puck not bounced off the thigh of Columbus Blue Jackets defenseman Zach Werenski and then deflected off Capitals center Lars Eller in the second overtime of Game 3, a wacky bounce that lifted Washington to its first playoff win. He secured the Capitals' last playoff win, too, recognizing that a puck had squeaked through Vegas goaltender Marc-Andre Fleury. Eller got his stick behind Fleury and swatted the puck into the net, the decisive goal with 7:37 remaining that lifted Washington to a 4-3 lead.

The rest was up to goaltender Braden Holtby. He wasn't the starter when these playoffs began, supplanted by Philipp Grubauer because Holtby had struggled in the second half of the season. He reclaimed the net as the starter in Game 3 of the Capitals' first-round series, when Washington was facing a two-game deficit after losing the first two contests at home. His redemption story modeled his team's, rallying when he seemed down and out.

For all of Washington's bumps throughout the season — and there were definitely more bumps this year — the team was able to consistently pick itself back up. The first 20 games had been an exercise in that, getting over the grief from another devastating early playoff exit. "If you look at our playoff records and how we've been, it can't get any worse," Backstrom said in late March.

With the puck iced and less than a second left, Ovechkin took off his helmet, anticipating the celebration that was to come. He started jumping. On the ice, he found Backstrom, pulling him into a long embrace as they screamed in each other's face.

It can't get any better.

Lars Eller got behind Vegas goaltender Marc-Andre Fleury and scored the series-winning goal. (PHOTO BY JOHN MCDONNELL)

CHAMPIONS
WASHINGTON
capitals
CCM

EASTERN CONFERENCE FINALS

CAPITALS 4, LIGHTNING 3

Finals, finally

BY BARRY SVRLUGA

Alex Ovechkin and John Carlson embraced after helping Washington reach its first Stanley Cup finals in 20 years. (PHOTO BY JONATHAN NEWTON)

Take the available information on the Washington Capitals — the way they perform when they lead in a playoff series, how they execute in seventh and deciding games, all the synonyms for "choking" that exist — and toss it in the trash. Crumple it up. Send it to the shredder. It's no longer relevant.

Washington's sporting reality changed Wednesday night. All the ghosts that used to hide in the corners? Well, someone finally turned on the lights, scared them away, and look what was revealed: a Game 7 performance that was, essentially, the opposite of so many of its predecessors. The authors were these new Capitals who have revealed themselves, bit by bit, as a group that stiffens when others — so many others — shrank.

That team is going to the Stanley Cup finals to play the Vegas Golden Knights because of that quality over all others. That team beat the Tampa Bay Lightning, 4-0, in Game 7 of the Eastern Conference finals Wednesday night. That team delivered what is, without argument, the most significant victory in the history of a National Hockey League franchise that for so long has been a constant source of misery for folks who care and an easy mark to be mocked by those who don't.

What just happened?

"Nothing's easy," owner Ted Leonsis said after he emerged from a locker room that was both jubilant and businesslike. "Nothing's given to you. I'm really pleased with the demeanor that I saw in the locker room. While they're happy, we want to win a Cup."

But for now, soak in this night, because there hasn't been one like it in 20 years. Soak in Alex Ovechkin, skating into the pile of white jerseys when the final horn sounded. All the agony and antacids from the past decade and more, they all seemed worth it in that moment.

"The emotion," Ovechkin said. "It's hard to explain how I feel."

He spoke as the captain, the superstar. He could have been speaking for the entirety of the Capitals fan base, bruised over generations, buoyant on this night.

To reach the Stanley Cup finals, the Capitals received both the expected — a trademark goal from Ovechkin, a stellar performance from goaltender Braden Holtby, who closed the series with back-to-back shutouts — and the out-of-the-blue, a pair of goals from forward Andre Burakovsky, who was benched only two games earlier. That improbable combination is what it took to unburden themselves — and more importantly, their fans — of so much baggage accumulated over the years. That repeated blunt-force trauma required fans to ask difficult questions about their investment of emotions, of finances, of time: Why do I do this?

This is why. Wednesday night is why. An entire group of Capitals pushing the goal off its posts and hugging, jumping in unison — that's why.

There is another step, for sure, because the Golden Knights await in the finals — the first time in the championship round for one of Washington's four major pro teams since 1998. Then, the Capitals were swept away by the far superior Detroit Red Wings. That's a high point?

Wednesday night, now that felt more like a franchise on its way to the apex. Consider how these Capitals handled themselves not only in winning the final two games of this series 7-0, but also what transpired Wednesday night alone. Ovechkin, the symbol both of Washington's rise as an annual contender and its failures when the playoffs began, scored just 62 seconds after the puck dropped. The feelings that this night would be different began right there.

Or maybe they just continued. The truth is, this team hasn't felt like the others, the groups that crumbled. That didn't guarantee anything against a Tampa Bay team that was better in the regular season, that had earned the top seed in the Eastern Conference. But it did mean something about how the Capitals evaluated themselves.

"I think our group here really understands what it means to be a team and how to win," Holtby said. "Maybe in the past we've had more skill, were better on paper, whatever. But this team, everyone knows their role, everyone can pitch in, everyone's comfortable with each other. I haven't been on a team like this where in any situation we're confident in each other, don't get down on each other. It's a strong group. That's extremely hard to come by."

He's talking about the Capitals, right?

There were other indications Wednesday would be a milestone. In the first period, Tampa Bay's Anthony Cirelli whiffed on a puck that just sat in front of the net, begging to go in. Early in the second, Lightning forward Yanni Gourde did the same. Burakovsky's confidence was so shot before the sixth game of this series that he said he needed to hire a sports psychologist. That's the guy who takes advantage of an errant puck and created a 2-0 lead? And then added another?

For the Capitals, this is through-the-looking-glass material. And it happened when it mattered most. What world are we living in? Flip-flop the jerseys on the two teams, then take the bounces and breaks into consideration, and a true Capitals fan might have believed what happened Wednesday night — because it always happened to them. This? This might take clipping out the box score, framing it behind museum-quality glass and hanging it on the wall to believe that it transpired.

"Sometimes you have to deserve it," Ovechkin said, "and sometimes luck have to be on your side."

For once, both were true for the Capitals. They deserved it. And they got a bounce or two.

Because, when the disappointments rolled in like clockwork each May, we recounted those that went before them, it's worth recalling them now — and then dismissing them outright. The Capitals' Game 7s from recent history had provided some of the most significant gut punches the franchise can produce — a year ago against Pittsburgh, three straight times against the New York Rangers, Montreal and Pittsburgh again. They run together.

At some point, all of those results add up. They wear on fans. They become part of the fabric.

Until a group of guys comes along and takes out all the stitches, one by one.

"These whole playoffs," center Nicklas Backstrom said, "we've played with a different confidence than previous years."

They're also at a different point in their development than the only other Capitals team to reach the finals. Those Capitals of Peter Bondra and Olaf Kolzig and Dale Hunter had finished last the previous year and would miss the playoffs the next year. They reached the 1998 finals almost on a lark.

This group has been building to this point for more than a decade. Being lousy year after year brings no pressure. Winning eight division titles in 11 seasons, taking three Presidents' Trophies as the league's best regular season team — that brings real expectations, not to mention the worst kind of disappointment when each season ends with a loss.

Wednesday night, though, they won. They won in a situation in which other Capitals teams have folded. They won in a way that demonstrated how different they have become. Thus, they have guaranteed themselves the chance to end their season with a victory, hoisting a Cup.

This is the Capitals we're talking about, right? Watch the tape again to be certain. Sure seems like a different team.

WASHINGTON
capitals
BAUER
CCM
PANY
LAKEWOO
RANCH

GAME 1

CAPITALS 4, LIGHTNING 2

Capitals bury Bolts beneath early goals

BY ISABELLE KHURSHUDYAN

Alex Ovechkin celebrates Michal Kempny's first-period goal. Ovechkin added a key score of his own to close the first 20 minutes as Washington built a 4-0 lead and held on to win the series opener. (PHOTO BY JONATHAN NEWTON)

MAY 11 AT TAMPA BAY

Washington	**2**	**2**	**0**	**4**
Tampa Bay	**0**	**0**	**2**	**2**

FIRST PERIOD

Scoring: 1, Washington, Kempny 1 (Carlson, Kuznetsov), 7:28. 2, Washington, Ovechkin 9 (Kuznetsov, Oshie), 19:54 (pp).

SECOND PERIOD

Scoring: 3, Washington, Beagle 2 (Orlov, Connolly), 2:40. 4, Washington, Eller 4 (Oshie, Ovechkin), 6:42 (pp).

THIRD PERIOD

Scoring: 5, Tampa Bay, Stamkos 4 (Hedman, Kucherov), 3:45 (pp). 6, Tampa Bay, Palat 5 (Johnson, Stralman), 13:03.

SHOTS ON GOAL

Washington	9	16	7	32
Tampa Bay	2	8	11	21

Power-play opportunities:
Washington 2 of 4; Tampa Bay 1 of 3.

Goalies: Washington, Holtby 9-3 (21 shots-19 saves). Tampa Bay, Vasilevskiy 8-3 (25-21), Domingue 0-0 (7-7).

The paddle-shaped rattlers thundered throughout Amalie Arena as the puck dropped Friday night. But with each minute that ticked by, the Tampa Bay Lightning's side of the scoreboard seemingly frozen at zero shots on goal, the drumming subsided. More than nine minutes passed before the Lightning had a shot on goal, and the Washington Capitals had the lead by then. Not long after Tampa Bay's third shot came Washington's third goal, the contest stunningly lopsided — especially considering the Lightning entered the series as the heavy favorite.

Just four days after one of the biggest wins in franchise history, one that clinched their first Eastern Conference finals berth in 20 years and vanquished a heated rival, the Capitals responded with one of their more impressive wins of the postseason, a 4-2 dismantling of the Lightning.

"One thing we really wanted to focus on was to not have a letdown after, obviously, there's a lot of emotions through our locker room after that series win," goaltender Braden Holtby said of the Capitals' 2-1 overtime win Monday night that eliminated the host Pittsburgh Penguins, who claimed the Stanley Cup the past two seasons. "You enjoy it while it's there, but we had a couple days to just refocus, put it out of our mind and scout the Lightning to see what we could do to have success against them. ... I think we just went right back to work, and I thought the guys responded really well to this game."

For the second straight game, Washington's strong defensive play overcame the absence of top center Nicklas Backstrom, who's out with an injury to his right hand. The Capitals allowed the Lightning just two shots on goal in the first period as they took a two-goal lead. Washington had four goals to Tampa Bay's four shots less than seven minutes into the second period, with the Lightning suffocated by the Capitals' tight checking.

"It's throughout the whole lineup is where the strength is," forward T.J. Oshie said. "When you have one line after another, whether it's [Evgeny Kuznetsov's] line or [Jay Beagle's] line, coming in to the [defensive] zone and playing the same way, it just makes things so much easier. We get the puck back quicker, and we get to play offense a lot more."

A five-second sequence at the end of the first period took the Capitals from tied with the Lightning at intermission to up by two goals. Tampa Bay sniper Nikita Kucherov caught Washington out of position, getting behind defenseman Dmitry Orlov for a partial breakaway on Holtby. He scored a highlight-reel goal, tying the score at 1 with less than 10 seconds left, but a penalty was called before Kucherov's shot: The Lightning had six skaters on the ice.

That wiped Kucherov's goal off the board, and it put the Capitals on their first power play. As Tampa Bay cruised to the Eastern Conference finals, winning both of its first two series in five games, its penalty kill was a weakness: Entering Friday, the Lightning had yielded eight goals in 31 times shorthanded. Oshie won the first faceoff, pulling the puck back to Kuznetsov, who set up Alex Ovechkin. His blast from the point beat Tampa Bay goaltender Andrei Vasilevskiy for a 2-0 lead.

"It was a big moment for us," Coach Barry Trotz said. "That was a window of opportunity for us, and we were able to do something with it. In the playoffs, a lot of times you may get only one or two a game, and that was one of those windows that we were able to execute on and take advantage of."

The Capitals then got some fortunate breaks. After Orlov kept an offensive-zone shift alive, forward Brett Connolly flubbed a shot from point-blank range. But the puck took a lucky bounce off Tampa Bay defenseman Braydon Coburn's skate and onto Beagle's stick. He jammed it through Vasilevskiy's legs for a 3-0 lead 2:40 into the second period. Four minutes later, after arguably a soft roughing call on Kucherov, Washington's power play again took advantage. Lars Eller was promoted to the top unit with Backstrom out, and he scored on a rebound of Oshie's shot to make it 4-0.

At even strength, Eller centered the second line with Oshie and Jakub Vrana. Rookie Chandler Stephenson moved from the wing to center the third line with Connolly and left wing Andre Burakovsky, back after missing the past 10 playoff games with an upper-body injury. Though Backstrom is considered Washington's best two-way center, the Capitals held the Lightning to 10 shots through 40 minutes. Tampa Bay pulled

Vasilevskiy at second intermission in favor of backup Louis Domingue and then scored twice in the third period, but it couldn't overcome Washington's four-goal cushion.

"Guys are stepping up," said Holtby, who made 19 saves. "We know probably better than anyone how complete a player Nick is, especially defensively. There's a ton of things that don't get noticed except for from us. I think our guys respect Nick so much that we know we have to step up because he's a huge spot to fill and our guys are doing a phenomenal job, especially up the middle."

Offseason turnover because of salary cap constraints and the Vegas expansion draft had made defense Washington's greatest weakness during the regular season. The turning point came at the trade deadline, when the team acquired defenseman Michal Kempny, who moved into a top-four role beside top right-shot John Carlson. And on Friday night, with Ovechkin battling defensemen Victor Hedman and Dan Girardi for position in front of Vasilevskiy 7:28 into the game, Kempny's shot from the left point got through the traffic for Washington's first goal.

Not long after the Capitals' acquisitions of Kempny and depth defenseman Jakub Jerabek, the team had a meeting to address its defensive-zone protocols, clarifying certain terminology and reemphasizing the team's basic philosophy of defending as a five-man group. Oshie felt that, perhaps because the Capitals had struggled with their play away from the puck all year, they had become a better defensive team than ever by the time the postseason started.

Missing a key offensive cog Friday night — Backstrom had a solo conditioning skate Thursday with some light stickhandling, an encouraging sign — the Capitals used impressive defensive play to control puck possession and score off that.

Now they have early control of the series with a Stanley Cup finals appearance at stake — and one of their best players could be back in the lineup soon.

Alex Ovechkin had three hits, including this one on Lightning defenseman Victor Hedman, to go along with a goal and an assist. (PHOTO BY JONATHAN NEWTON)

BAY
WASHINGTON
Capitals
CCM

GAME 2

CAPITALS 6, LIGHTNING 2

Capitals continue to dominate on the road

BY ISABELLE KHURSHUDYAN

The Caps, taking the ice for warmups, scored the final five goals of the game to take a 2-0 lead with the series returning to Washington. (PHOTO BY JONATHAN NEWTON)

MAY 13 AT TAMPA BAY

Washington	**1**	**3**	**2**	**6**
Tampa Bay	**2**	**0**	**0**	**2**

FIRST PERIOD

Scoring: 1, Washington, Wilson 3 (Niskanen, Kuznetsov), 0:28. 2, Tampa Bay, Point 5 (Hedman, Stamkos), 7:08 (pp). 3, Tampa Bay, Stamkos 5 (Kucherov, Point), 10:22 (pp).

SECOND PERIOD

Scoring: 4, Washington, Smith-Pelly 3 (Chiasson, Carlson), 2:50. 5, Washington, Eller 5 (Vrana), 18:58. 6, Washington, Kuznetsov 8 (Eller, Ovechkin), 19:57 (pp).

THIRD PERIOD

Scoring: 7, Washington, Ovechkin 10 (Wilson, Kuznetsov), 3:34. 8, Washington, Connolly 3 (Eller, Carlson), 12:57.

SHOTS ON GOAL

Washington	10	13	14	37
Tampa Bay	13	8	14	35

Power-play opportunities: Washington 1 of 3; Tampa Bay 2 of 4.

Goalies: Washington, Holtby 10-3 (35 shots-33 saves). Tampa Bay, Vasilevskiy 8-4 (37-31).

The Washington Capitals have developed a tradition — born out of superstition — for their road playoff games. A morning skate can't start without captain Alex Ovechkin sprinting around the rink, a solo lap to the sound of sticks tapping from his teammates, hockey's version of cheering. Once Ovechkin goes all the way around, the rest of the team hops onto the ice to join him.

With one road win after another, the Capitals have kept the ritual going. And for a second straight game at Amalie Arena, Ovechkin could be found fist-bumping, celebrating a key goal and looking right at home in the opposition's arena. Washington beat the Tampa Bay Lightning, 6-2, on Sunday in Game 2 of the Eastern Conference finals, and the Capitals have a commanding two-games-to-none series lead with the next two games at Washington's Capital One Arena on Tuesday and Thursday.

Against a team that won more games than any other in the NHL this season, the Capitals improbably have dominated play through two games while overcoming an injury to one of their best players. On Sunday night, they also had to weather some questionable officiating early in the game. One thing they have had going for them all postseason: They are 7-1 on the road.

"I feel like we spend much more time together on the road, and it show up in our game," said center Evgeny Kuznetsov, who finished with a goal and two assists. "But overall for us, it doesn't matter where we play, who we play against. It's our game."

Players suggested that perhaps Washington's game gets simpler on the road, when the opposing team has more control of the matchups with the last change. The Capitals might not feel as much pressure as they do in front of their home fans. Maybe that's why Washington has been able to continue winning even as top center Nicklas Backstrom has missed three games with a right hand injury.

Lars Eller has seen an uptick in minutes and responsibility with Backstrom out, anchoring wingers T.J. Oshie and Jakub Vrana as well as moving onto the top power-play unit. He also is one of the Capitals' top penalty killers. He has thrived in the bigger role, and with Sunday's game tied, Eller redirected Vrana's centering pass to lift Washington to a 3-2 lead with just 1:02 left in the second period. Eller has six points in the past four games, and he has been playing among the most minutes of Washington's forwards with Backstrom out. "I embrace when there's more on the line and the stakes are higher," Eller said. "I always like that, and I think that it brings out the best in me. Now with Nick out, I've just been playing more minutes. The role is not that much different; I think it's just I'm out there more."

Less than a minute after his goal, Eller took a key power-play draw for the Capitals. Lightning goaltender Andrei Vasilevskiy had been whistled for tripping forward Andre Burakovsky, putting Washington on the power play with less than 10 seconds left before intermission. Two nights earlier, the Capitals had executed a play off a man-advantage for a goal with less than eight seconds left in a period. They pulled it off again after Eller won the faceoff. Kuznetsov collected the rebound from Ovechkin's shot, and Kuznetsov's shot from the half wall went off the stick of Lightning defenseman Ryan McDonagh and under Vasilevskiy's pad with less than three seconds to play.

"You'd think we'd learn from our mistake in Game 1," Lightning captain Steven Stamkos said, "but they get one, and that's really a killer going down 4-2 instead of 3-2. It's little details of the game at this time of the year, and they've executed, and we haven't."

After those two goals in the last 1:02 of the second period, Washington piled it on in the third with goals from Ovechkin and Brett Connolly, a former Lightning player. By the time the game was over, the specks of fans wearing Washington red seemed more prominent because so many wearing Tampa Bay blue had bolted for the exits.

"They look like they're frustrated a little but over there," Connolly said.

Though Kuznetsov's power-play goal was the game's turning point, the Capitals fumed over a pair of calls that went against them in the first period. Tom Wilson redirected in a Matt Niskanen shot to give Washington a 1-0 lead just 28 seconds into the game, but then Wilson tumbled into Vasilevskiy less than seven minutes later. He was assessed a goaltender interference penalty, though the Capitals argued that Lightning

Lars Eller, third from left, put Washington ahead for good in the second period. (PHOTO BY JONATHAN NEWTON)

forward Chris Kunitz hooked Wilson as he was driving the net and that's what caused Wilson to fall into Vasilevskiy.

Just 20 seconds into the power play, Niskanen blocked a pass from Stamkos, but the puck bounced off Niskanen's skate and right to Brayden Point in the high slot. With goaltender Braden Holtby still turned toward Stamkos, Point had a wide-open net and didn't miss, tying the game 7:08 into the first period.

Though the penalty call on Wilson was questionable, the next infraction assessed on Washington was clearly an incorrect one by the officials. Less than two minutes after Point's goal, Oshie was called for high-sticking Victor Hedman. Ovechkin immediately objected, skating over to the referee to voice his displeasure. A video replay showed that Hedman actually was clipped by a puck in the face, not Oshie's stick, but the call stood anyway. Ovechkin started sarcastically clapping on the ice.

"They're not going to reverse it," Connolly said. "[The officials] knew after. I'm sure they saw it. But sometimes you've just got to go up to the ref and say, 'Hey, it's okay. It's fine.' It happens, and we just kept pushing."

Though the Tampa Bay power play scored again to lift the Lightning to a 2-1 lead at 10:22, the Capitals recognized that they had outplayed Tampa Bay at even strength to that point. That paid off less than three minutes into the second period, when fourth-liners Alex Chiasson and Devante Smith-Pelly had a two-on-one. Chiasson's pass went off Tampa Bay defenseman Mikhail Sergachev's stick, but Smith-Pelly still corralled the puck to shoot it past Vasilevskiy and tie the game.

And then the Capitals settled into their road routine as if they were right at home.

"I can't wait to go home and play the game," Ovechkin said. "The fans are going to be all over the place, and we've waited for this moment for a long time. It's going to be pretty cool and pretty special."

GAME 3

LIGHTNING 4, CAPITALS 2

Put the broom back in the closet

BY ISABELLE KHURSHUDYAN

There was a broom at the Washington Capitals' practice facility Tuesday morning. A group of overeager fans asked injured center Nicklas Backstrom to sign it, hopeful for a sweep in the Eastern Conference finals against the Tampa Bay Lightning.

Though Washington remains in control of the series, the Capitals' 4-2 loss to the Lightning in Game 3 ensured this won't be a sweep, not that the team ever really expected the matchup to be easy. Players anticipated a desperate Tampa Bay team on Tuesday night at Capital One Arena after the Lightning dropped the first two games of the series in its home arena. Costly penalties and a leaky penalty kill just made it a little easier for Tampa Bay to take the third game and cut Washington's lead in this best-of-seven series to 2-1.

"No one expected 4-0, right?" Capitals center Evgeny Kuznetsov said. "We all know it's going to be a tough series. We just have to relax a little bit and stay positive. It's still fun."

Though teams have a 21-0 series record when they have won the first two games on the road in the final two rounds of the Stanley Cup playoffs, the Capitals know how quickly things can change. They fell into a two-games-to-none hole after losing both games in Washington in the first round against Columbus, but then reeled off four straight wins. The Capitals expected a Lightning squad that won the most games in the NHL during the regular season to respond in Game 3, and for the first time in the series, Tampa Bay scored the first goal.

Goaltender Braden Holtby was called for tripping Tampa Bay forward Yanni Gourde, and after defenseman Brooks Orpik whiffed on his attempt to clear the puck out of the Washington zone, the puck made its way to center Steven Stamkos in the left faceoff circle. His one-timer was a laser, a shot Holtby had no chance of stopping.

On Tuesday morning, Tampa Bay Coach Jon Cooper lamented how little his team had played with the lead through the first two games. Washington had been starting strong throughout the playoffs, scoring first in all but three of its postseason games entering Game 3.

"You have to make them play catch-up because when they do have the lead, they sit back," Cooper said before the game. "You have to go through four guys. They all can skate, they're all angling, they're all in lanes, and it just makes it tougher. When they don't have the lead, they're a little bit more loose in the way they play. They don't sit back as much. They're not waiting for you to make a mistake because they're trying to create offense themselves. If you want to have a chance to open things up for yourself, make sure you get the lead."

The Lightning was able to do just that thanks to its power play. Less than two minutes into the second period, Capitals center Lars Eller was called for closing his hand on the puck, and it was a one-timer from the opposite circle that got past Holtby this time. Defenseman Victor Hedman set up a Nikita Kucherov one-timer to lift Tampa Bay to a 2-0 lead, the Lightning's first edge of more than one goal in the series.

"It's kind of like we have [Alex Ovechkin] on that one side, and they kind of have it on both sides" with Stamkos and Kucherov, Orpik said. "You take one guy away, and it leaves the other guy open."

For Washington, Eller's infraction marked a 60th minor penalty in these playoffs, which is a postseason high. Because the puck movement on the Lightning's power play has given the Capitals fits, discipline becomes even more important. Though Tampa Bay's power play had been overshadowed by Washington's in the first two games, the Lightning scored three goals on seven opportunities. It was 2 for 5 on Tuesday night, which meant it got too many looks in Coach Barry Trotz's opinion.

"To get back in a game, it took a lot of flow out of our game," Trotz said.

Less than two minutes after Kucherov's power-play goal, Hedman made it a three-goal deficit for Washington with just the second even-strength goal Tampa Bay has scored in the series. A home arena that had been anxious for its first conference finals game in 20 years deflated.

Meanwhile, the Capitals' power play, hot all postseason with a goal in all but two games entering Game 3, couldn't convert. Brett Connolly narrowed the deficit with his wrister midway through the second period, and that seemed to shift momentum in Washington's favor. The Capitals got a power play less than three minutes later, but Lightning goaltender Andrei Vasilevskiy stopped all three shots he faced during it. Brayden Point's shot through Chandler Stephenson's legs then made it a 4-1 game before second intermission.

"I don't think they were more desperate," Ovechkin said. "They just scored power-play goals, and we didn't."

The pushback from Tampa Bay was expected, and though Washington couldn't match on Tuesday night, the margin for error will be slimmer in Thursday's Game 4, when the Capitals would prefer to push the Lightning to the brink of elimination rather than return to Tampa Bay with the series tied.

"Nobody said it was going to be easy," Ovechkin said. "We was ready for it, and nobody going to give up."

MAY 15 AT WASHINGTON

Tampa Bay	**1**	**3**	**0**	**4**
Washington	**0**	**1**	**1**	**2**

FIRST PERIOD

Scoring: 1, Tampa Bay, Stamkos 6 (Point, Hedman), 13:53 (pp).

SECOND PERIOD

Scoring: 2, Tampa Bay, Kucherov 7 (Stamkos, Hedman), 1:50 (pp). 3, Tampa Bay, Hedman 1 (Palat, Kucherov), 3:37. 4, Washington, Connolly 4 (Stephenson, Niskanen), 10:31. 5, Tampa Bay, Point 6 (Johnson, Coburn), 16:03.

THIRD PERIOD

Scoring: 6, Washington, Kuznetsov 9 (Oshie, Eller), 16:58.

SHOTS ON GOAL

Tampa Bay	10	8	5	23
Washington	14	11	13	38

Power-play opportunities: Tampa Bay 2 of 5; Washington 0 of 3.

Goalies: Tampa Bay, Vasilevskiy 9-4 (38 shots-36 saves). Washington, Holtby 10-4 (23-19).

Alex Ovechkin and the Caps returned home for Game 3, but the Lightning got its first win in the series. (PHOTO BY TONI L. SANDYS)

GAME 4

LIGHTNING 4, CAPITALS 2

Trouble at home: Caps falter again

BY ISABELLE KHURSHUDYAN

With a second left in regulation, the goal light above the Washington Capitals' net flashing once again, Alex Ovechkin's frustration boiled over. He snapped his stick in half against the cage's crossbar. Then he took the half in his hand and broke that into two pieces. The fragment that remained in hands he soon threw against the boards, the final phase of demolishing the twig that had failed him all night.

Though Washington largely dominated play, launching 38 pucks toward Lightning goaltender Andrei Vasilevskiy, the Capitals lost a second straight home game, 4-2, squandering a golden opportunity to take control of the best-of-seven Eastern Conference finals. Washington came to Capital One Arena with a 2-0 lead, and now the series is tied with two of the next three games in Tampa.

"Yeah, of course, it's a missed opportunity," Ovechkin said. "It is what it is. Nothing we can do. We're not going to look back. We're just going to look forward. This group of guys has been in different situations all year, and we fight through it. So, it's a huge test. We're still going to have fun, we're still going to enjoy it and we'll see what happens. We're going to Tampa and play our game and try to get a victory and come back home."

Midway through the final period, the Capitals had just done what had seemed impossible at times: survive a Lightning power play. Capital One Arena roared. A moment later, it fell into a stunned silence. The red goal light flashed, and goaltender Braden Holtby was sprawled across his crease. Just six seconds after the power play ended, Tampa Bay forward Alex Killorn drove the net and wedged a puck through Holtby as the netminder challenged him.

Killorn's goal, with 8:03 remaining in the third period, gave the Lightning a 3-2 lead. Tampa Bay then added an empty-net tally with 1.5 seconds left before the final horn.

"Play was still in our end, so as a goalie, you don't even really know if power play is killed off or not," Holtby said of Killorn's goal. "You're just trying to do your job, and I think it's a play that, once I watch, I'll realize that I could do a better job on. Not the time of the game that I want to give up a goal. Analyze it, figure out what are the things you could do better, and you move forward."

Capitals top center Nicklas Backstrom returned to the lineup after missing four playoff games with a right hand injury, and that meant Washington had its entire roster healthy and available for the first time since Game 2 of the team's first-round series against Columbus. But it didn't matter with Vasilevskiy saving his best game of the series for Thursday night, when he made 36 saves. Before Killorn's game-winning goal, Vasilevskiy bought time for his teammates.

After a disappointing first period, the Capitals made a push in the second. Less than six minutes into the period, Ovechkin's backhand saucer pass through the neutral zone hit center Evgeny Kuznetsov in stride for a breakaway, and he beat Vasilevskiy with a shot through the goaltender's legs.

But Vasilevskiy was the difference for the rest of the period, keeping the game tied at 2 despite Washington controlling play. The Lightning had a 20-minute stretch from the first period to midway through the second without a single shot on goal, and by the time both teams got through 40 minutes, the Capitals had 29 shots to Tampa Bay's 13.

With nine minutes left in the frame, Ovechkin had a glorious chance at point-blank range, but his shot sailed over the net. He kicked up a leg, hung his head back and screamed in frustration.

"After the second it was, I don't want to say frustrating to come out only tied, but I think we missed maybe a few opportunities there," defenseman John Carlson said.

Less than six minutes into the third period, Chandler Stephenson's centering pass bounced off Lightning defenseman Victor Hedman and fluttered toward Brett Connolly, who managed to deflect the puck forward with the shaft of his stick. Vasilevskiy swatted at the puck with his glove to keep the puck out of the net. He looked like a typical hot goalie poised to steal his team a game.

Then the Lightning power play, which is 6 for 14 this series, got an opportunity with 10:09 left in the game after center Lars Eller was called for his second penalty of the contest and his fifth infraction in the past two games. Washington managed to kill off his hooking minor, but Tampa Bay maintained possession, and, moments after the teams were back at even strength, Killorn got a shot behind Holtby from close range.

Three shifts after defenseman Dmitry Orlov scored Washington's first goal, Tampa Bay responded, capitalizing on an egregious blind, backhand pass across the slot by Capitals defenseman Michal Kempny. The Lightning took the turnover gift, and Brayden Point completed a tic-tac-toe passing sequence with a tap-in goal to tie the game. Less than three minutes later, Eller was called for slashing.

Tampa Bay's power play has given Washington fits this series. While the Capitals have Ovechkin firing one-timers from the left faceoff circle, the Lightning has Stamkos and Nikita Kucherov doing that from each side. Point collected a puck in front of the net and fed Stamkos on the left side, where he was all alone and easily beat Holtby to give Tampa Bay a 2-1 lead.

The efficiency of the Lightning's power play then made Washington's man-advantage look worse as the Capitals got three straight power plays in the final nine minutes of the first period. Vasilevskiy made seven saves, three of which were on Ovechkin. The more opportunities the Capitals got, the worse their power play performed.

The Lightning's penalty kill was considered a weakness entering this series, and the Capitals had dinged the unit for three power-play goals through the first two games. Washington is 0 for 7 since.

"We lost the battle again," Ovechkin said. "They scored two goals. We didn't."

By the time Anthony Cirelli scored the empty-netter in the waning moments, more than a few boos could be heard from the fans who remained.

"Our intention is to go on the road and win a game in Tampa," Capitals Coach Barry Trotz said. "We've already done that twice."

MAY 17 AT WASHINGTON

Tampa Bay	**2**	**0**	**2**	**4**
Washington	**1**	**1**	**0**	**2**

FIRST PERIOD

Scoring: 1, Washington, Orlov 2 (Niskanen, Oshie), 4:28. 2, Tampa Bay, Point 7 (Gourde, Johnson), 5:38. 3, Tampa Bay, Stamkos 7 (Miller, Point), 8:32 (pp).

SECOND PERIOD

Scoring: 4, Washington, Kuznetsov 10 (Ovechkin, Wilson), 5:18.

THIRD PERIOD

Scoring: 5, Tampa Bay, Killorn 5 (Palat, Sergachev), 11:57. 6, Tampa Bay, Cirelli 2, 19:58 (en).

SHOTS ON GOAL

Tampa Bay	7	6	7	20
Washington	15	14	9	38

Power-play opportunities: Tampa Bay 1 of 2; Washington 0 of 4.

Goalies: Tampa Bay, Vasilevskiy 10-4 (38 shots-36 saves). Washington, Holtby 10-5 (19-16).

Alex Ovechkin bashed his stick on the goal cage after losing Game 4. (PHOTO BY TONI L. SANDYS)

GAME 5

LIGHTNING 3, CAPITALS 2

Three quick strikes, and nearly out

BY ISABELLE KHURSHUDYAN

It was vintage Alex Ovechkin, a one-timer from the left side of the offensive zone that had so often injected life into his Washington Capitals. This one buzzed past Tampa Bay Lightning goalie Andrei Vasilevskiy and fluttered the back of the net. The problem was that there was just 1:36 left in the game, and it cut Washington's deficit from two goals to one. The Capitals returned to their bench for a brief timeout, a conference for a final push. It was all too little and much too late.

Washington fell into an early hole and never climbed out of it in a 3-2 Game 5 loss. Now the Capitals face another deficit, down 3-2 in this best-of-seven Eastern Conference finals. After winning the first two games of the series they have lost three straight, and one more will end their season.

Twenty-one teams have won the first two games of a best-of-seven conference finals or Stanley Cup finals on the road in the past 50 years. All 21 went on to win the series. None of those series lasted more than six games, and if Washington advances, it will have to be with a Game 7 win in Tampa.

But before the Capitals can get there, they will have to reconcile how they started this game so poorly, yielding three goals in the first 21 minutes.

"It's unexplainable, obviously," center Jay Beagle said.

"We ended up on our heels, not executing, not playing quick, and dug ourselves a hole," Coach Barry Trotz said.

Down two goals after an abysmal first period, Washington dug itself into a bigger hole by allowing the Lightning's fourth line to score 33 seconds out of intermission. Defenseman Anton Stralman skated up the ice and drove the net. Winger Ryan Callahan crashed the net, and the rebound from Stralman's shot went off Callahan's glove to get past goaltender Braden Holtby. That gave the Lightning a 3-0 lead, and Tampa Bay had twice struck in the opening minute of a period.

"We stunk in the first," defenseman Matt Niskanen said. "They just outskated us, outbattled us, and the first shift in the second, I just get burned wide and they get another one."

Niskanen ultimately took the blame for all three Tampa Bay goals. The Lightning's fourth line came into the game having combined for two points among center Cedric Paquette, Chris Kunitz and Callahan in the postseason. By the end of the game the trio had two goals and had slowed down Ovechkin, who was held without a single shot on goal through two periods.

The Capitals were feeling positive as the series returned to Amalie Arena. Trotz said he felt his team had been the better one in three out of the first four games. As the team took the ice for Thursday's morning skate, players laughed and joked around, seemingly loose. Washington entered Game 5 with a 7-1 record on the road in the postseason. The Capitals had won the first two games in Tampa thanks to fast starts, but that element was missing Saturday.

Just 19 seconds in, Paquette scored when some sloppy neutral-zone play by the Capitals allowed a two-on-one. Paquette intercepted defenseman Dmitry Orlov's pass to create the turnover, and Paquette was all alone as Callahan fed him the puck at the edge of the left faceoff circle.

The top defensive pairing of Orlov and Niskanen was involved in Tampa Bay's second goal, too. Orlov was carrying the puck at the Lightning's offensive blue line when Steven Stamkos dropped him, arguably a trip that went uncalled. Orlov lost the puck, and Nikita Kucherov got it to set up Ondrej Palat, who used a kneeling Niskanen as a screen on Holtby. That gave the Lightning a 2-0 lead 9:04 into the first period, injecting confidence into a Tampa Bay team that had struggled in this building during the first two games of the series.

"We've just got to keep our composure," Holtby said. "The second goal, obviously, we know it's a missed call. That doesn't happen if Orly doesn't get tripped. That's where we've done a really good job of regrouping."

After the Capitals finished with four shots in the first period — T.J. Oshie's wrister from 55 feet away from the net was the only shot from a forward in the opening 20 minutes — the Capitals controlled play for the majority of the second and third periods. Trotz was frustrated that the team still didn't draw a single power play all game. Washington finished with 30 shots to Tampa Bay's 22.

Trotz flipped centers Nicklas Backstrom and Evgeny Kuznetsov, moving Backstrom to the line with Ovechkin and right wing Tom Wilson. Less than five minutes into the second period, Kuznetsov tipped a Niskanen point shot to trim Tampa Bay's lead.

But the two-goal deficit proved too much to overcome in the third period, and for the first time this postseason, the Capitals are on the brink of elimination.

"I think it's important just to let them know we're not going anywhere," Oshie said. "They had a really good first period, but after that I think we really took it to them. Their goaltender made some big saves. We hit some posts. Not that we're going to lean on those and feel bad for ourselves, but I think we can feel confident going into the next game where if we've got everyone playing, we're going to do a good job."

MAY 19 AT TAMPA BAY

Washington	**0**	**1**	**1**	**2**
Tampa Bay	**2**	**1**	**0**	**3**

FIRST PERIOD

Scoring: 1, Tampa Bay, Paquette 1 (Callahan), 0:19. 2, Tampa Bay, Palat 6 (Kucherov), 9:04.

SECOND PERIOD

Scoring: 3, Tampa Bay, Callahan 2 (Stralman, Kunitz), 0:33. 4, Washington, Kuznetsov 11 (Oshie, Niskanen), 4:21.

THIRD PERIOD

Scoring: 5, Washington, Ovechkin 11 (Carlson, Eller), 18:24.

SHOTS ON GOAL

Washington	4	13	13	30
Tampa Bay	13	5	4	22

Power-play opportunities: Washington 0 of 0; Tampa Bay 0 of 1.

Goalies: Washington, Holtby 10-6 (22 shots-19 saves). Tampa Bay, Vasilevskiy 11-4 (30-28).

Evgeny Kuznetsov, checking Lightning center Brayden Point into the boards, scored in the second period, but the Caps fell short. (PHOTO BY TONI L. SANDYS)

GAME 6

CAPITALS 3, LIGHTNING 0

On home ice, series gets full extension

BY ISABELLE KHURSHUDYAN

T.J. Oshie's second-period goal was all the Capitals would need in Game 6. (PHOTO BY JONATHAN NEWTON)

MAY 21 AT WASHINGTON

Tampa Bay	**0**	**0**	**0**	**0**
Washington	**0**	**1**	**2**	**3**

FIRST PERIOD

Scoring: None.

SECOND PERIOD

Scoring: 1, Washington, Oshie 6 (Backstrom, Kuznetsov), 15:12 (pp).

THIRD PERIOD

Scoring: 2, Washington, Smith-Pelly 4 (Stephenson, Beagle), 10:02. 3, Washington, Oshie 7 (Backstrom), 19:10.

SHOTS ON GOAL

Tampa Bay	6	8	10	24
Washington .	8	15	11	34

Power-play opportunities: Tampa Bay 0 of 2; Washington 1 of 1.

Goalies: Tampa Bay, Vasilevskiy 11-5 (33 shots-31 saves). Washington, Holtby 11-6 (24-24).

The Washington Capitals' Stanley Cup hopes were revived by Alex Ovechkin bulldozing through bodies and by Braden Holtby standing tall in net, by Chandler Stephenson hustling down the ice to negate an icing call and by Devante Smith-Pelly perfectly placing a shot through Tampa Bay Lightning goaltender Andrei Vasilevskiy. This was Washington's most important game of the Stanley Cup playoffs — and of many players' careers — and the team dominated with a grit born out of urgency.

Capital One Arena's oft-angsty crowd started singing along to the White Stripes' "Seven Nation Army," its belief suddenly restored. These Capitals seem to save their best for when they are most desperate, and they staved off elimination in Game 6 of the Eastern Conference finals Monday night with a bruising, hard-earned, 3-0 win to force a Game 7 at Tampa Bay's Amalie Arena on Wednesday.

"Going into Game 7, I don't think I would want another — and I've been doing this for a while — I don't think there's a team I've ever had that I'd want to go into a Game 7 with," Coach Barry Trotz said. "This team has done a lot of special things this year. It's grown, and it continues to do that. What an opportunity going into Tampa. We've won on the road. We've won at home here. We'll see if we can earn the right to keep playing."

The Capitals checked the Lightning in every which way throughout the game. They got their first goal with their skill after they were rewarded with their first power play since Game 4. They scored on that lone opportunity, and they got insurance midway through the third period when Stephenson raced down the ice to fight off an icing call, backhanding the puck to a trailing Smith-Pelly in the slot. Washington ultimately didn't even need the extra cushion. Holtby saved his first shutout of the season, a flawless 24-save outing, for when the Capitals needed it most.

"It's the perfect time," Smith-Pelly said with a grin.

On Monday morning, Ovechkin said this was "probably" the most important game of his career. "It's two steps and you're in the Stanley Cup final," he said. As if to emphasize the point, he was a one-man wrecking ball to start the game. He knocked 6-foot-6 defenseman Victor Hedman off the puck — and then Yanni Gourde, too. Ovechkin crunched Chris Kunitz against the boards, and he leveled Braydon Coburn behind the net.

"When he's skating like that and trying to hit somebody, I'm pretty sure it's not really comfortable," line mate Evgeny Kuznetsov said.

Kuznetsov joked that he has "trucks" on both sides of him with Ovechkin and right wing Tom Wilson. Ovechkin had four hits through two periods, and Wilson and Brooks Orpik followed his lead with four more apiece. As the Capitals controlled play, they also made sure the Lightning felt them. When the final horn sounded, Washington had a 39-19 edge in hits, perhaps hoping to wear down Tampa Bay not only in this game, but for the next one, too.

"If it shows up in Game 7 where guys are starting to get tired, then it was all worth it," Smith-Pelly said.

"It's desperation really," Orpik said. "If you don't win tonight, you're not moving on. So you try to empty the tank as much as you can. That's one area where we have an edge, is our size and physical play. Over the course of a seven-game series, it's something we talk about. Take those opportunities. Don't get out of position. Try to wear them down when we can."

The physicality also energized a home crowd that the Capitals have struggled in front of this postseason. Washington was 3-5 at Capital One Arena before Monday night, and each big hit brought approval from the red-clad fans. The first goal of the game brought even more cheering.

Coming out of first intermission, Trotz had a word with the officials. Then Ovechkin skated over to conference with them. Washington had gone five full periods without a power play, and the team was clearly frustrated. Then, 13:49 into the second period,

Devante Smith-Pelly's third-period score gave Washington a two-goal cushion. (PHOTO BY JONATHAN NEWTON)

Coburn was called for hooking, and forward T.J. Oshie's one-timer from the slot beat Vasilevskiy 15:12 into the period to give Washington a 1-0 lead. For how frenetic the pace of play was, it was a surprisingly low-scoring game because of the excellent goaltending.

The Capitals have been bested by hot goaltenders in past postseasons, and Vasilevskiy looked poised to enter that lore early in Game 6. With less than a minute left in the opening period, Kuznetsov seemed to have Vasilevskiy beat with the puck in the crease and behind Vasilevskiy's pad. But Vasilevskiy sprawled across the blue paint and got his glove over in time to deny Kuznetsov's whack less than 10 feet away from the goal line.

Meanwhile, Holtby held his own at the opposite end. Through the first 12 games Holtby started this postseason, he had an impressive .928 save percentage and a 2.04 goals against average. But in Washington's previous three games entering Monday, all losses against the Lightning, Holtby had allowed 3.49 goals per game and posted an .844 save percentage, one of the reasons Tampa Bay was able to pull ahead in the series.

He wasn't tested much through two periods Monday, peppered with just 14 shots, but when the Lightning did get to him, he was sharp. On a Tampa Bay two-on-one 6:15 into the second period, Holtby expertly hugged the left side of his cage, and Anthony Cirelli had nowhere to place his backhand from point-blank range. With 13 minutes left in the third and the Capitals still ahead by only one, Holtby made a spectacular glove save on an Ondrej Palat slap shot while he was falling down.

A suddenly hopeful crowd chanted his name in appreciation.

"Fans weren't apprehensive," Trotz said. "We gave them something to cheer about."

MicroLu

GAME 7

CAPITALS 4, LIGHTNING 0

Cup finals for first time in two decades

BY ISABELLE KHURSHUDYAN

Tom Wilson pummeled Lightning defenseman Braydon Coburn, and Washington knocked out Tampa Bay. (PHOTO BY JONATHAN NEWTON)

MAY 23 AT TAMPA BAY

	1	2	3	T
Washington	**1**	**2**	**1**	**4**
Tampa Bay	**0**	**0**	**0**	**0**

FIRST PERIOD

Scoring: 1, Washington, Ovechkin 12 (Kuznetsov, Wilson), 1:02.

SECOND PERIOD

Scoring: 2, Washington, Burakovsky 1, 8:59. 3, Washington, Burakovsky 2 (Carlson), 16:31.

THIRD PERIOD

Scoring: 4, Washington, Backstrom 4, 16:17.

SHOTS ON GOAL

Washington	9	6	8	23
Tampa Bay	10	12	7	29

Power-play opportunities: Washington 0 of 2; Tampa Bay 0 of 1.

Goalies: Washington, Holtby 12-6 (29 shots-29 saves). Tampa Bay, Vasilevskiy 11-6 (22-19).

More than three minutes remained in the game, but Alex Ovechkin was on the bench, his gap-tooth smile unmistakable and wide. He raised both arms and hugged whoever was next to him. This Game 7 was a blowout, and he knew the history that had plagued him and his team was about to change.

Then 7.3 seconds remained, and Ovechkin stood in front of his bench and was wrapped in a few more embraces. Then time finally expired, and Ovechkin hopped off the bench and kicked up a leg before he was flanked by teammates Nicklas Backstrom and T.J. Oshie.

"You don't even have to say so much, you just have to look at each other," Backstrom said. "We've been waiting a long time for this."

Finally, Ovechkin grabbed the Prince of Wales Trophy for the Eastern Conference champions, unafraid of the superstition about not touching it, maybe because this team has already overcome so many odds. With the 4-0 win over the Tampa Bay Lightning in the deciding game of the Eastern Conference finals, Washington will play the Vegas Golden Knights in the Stanley Cup finals starting Monday in Nevada.

"Emotions?" Ovechkin said. "We're going to the Stanley Cup final. I think everybody happy, but we still have not finished. Not done yet, you know what I mean? I'm kind of emotional right now. It's hard to explain."

He struggled to collect his thoughts, smiling and shaking his head. Ovechkin then turned to goaltender Braden Holtby for help verbalizing the moment. Holtby smiled back at him. "You're doing great, babe," he told him.

"Finally, we get what we want," Ovechkin continued.

As Backstrom said earlier, "It only took 11 years."

The Capitals won this Game 7 with two goals from Andre Burakovsky, the inconsistent young winger who had been scratched just games earlier in this series and then admitted to needing to see a sports psychologist this season because he's often too hard on himself. They won Game 7 with Holtby pitching a second straight shutout, his only two of the season, after the goaltender had lost the starting job going into the playoffs. Washington won Game 7 with Ovechkin, the captain whose career has been associated with individual greatness but no significant team success, scoring the first goal of the game.

The Capitals have taken their hits and then hit right back all season, and perhaps no three players showed that better than the three who starred Wednesday night.

"I saw it all," Coach Barry Trotz said. "I saw it first shift. Ovi's been on a mission."

It took just 62 seconds for Ovechkin to make his mark on the game. On his first shift, center Evgeny Kuznetsov flicked a pass to him at the top of the left faceoff circle, and Ovechkin one-timed it, a fluttering, knuckling puck that got past Lightning goaltender Andrei Vasilevskiy. Ovechkin's career has been a highlight reel of laser shots like that one but also pained expressions in May.

The Capitals saw a more determined Ovechkin when he returned to Washington two weeks before the start of training camp, seemingly more dedicated to his offseason training. Then he started his assault on the NHL with a league-leading 49 goals. Earlier in this series, Lightning Coach Jon Cooper said he got the sense Ovechkin was taking out 13 years of frustration on one postseason. His first-period goal marked his 12th of these playoffs. "There were a lot of people doubting if he still had what it took," Trotz said. "The great players take exception to that. ... He said, 'I'm going to show you I'm still a great player.' And he did."

Just as the Capitals seemed on the brink of losing that one-goal lead to start the second period, center Lars Eller's chip into the offensive zone bounced off Lightning defenseman Dan Girardi, who had trouble corralling the puck. Burakovsky swiped it from him, dangled around him and then found the small hole between Vasilevskiy's elbow and pad to extend the Capitals' lead. That was just the team's second shot of the frame. All the while, Ovechkin was vocal on the bench, standing and yelling down the line.

When Burakovsky scored his second goal of the period, collecting John Carlson's bank pass off the boards before placing a shot through Vasilevskiy's legs, Ovechkin was waiting

to bump gloved fists with him on the bench. "[Expletive] right, baby," he yelled with a grin. "And then he said, 'Keep your shifts down a little bit,' so he was joking a little bit, too," Burakovsky said.

Devante Smith-Pelly had been knocked out for the game after taking a hit from Lightning defenseman Anton Stralman. Then Capitals blue-liner Brooks Orpik had to be helped off the ice after he was boarded by Cedric Paquette. But as has become this Washington team's identity, the Capitals embraced the adversity and pushed through it.

An offseason with the Vegas expansion draft and salary-cap constraints weakened the roster, veteran and skilled players replaced with rookies and inexpensive free agent additions. Defenseman Matt Niskanen recalled telling his wife before the season this team wasn't as good on paper, "but watch, this will be the year that we do something."

"I think our group here really understands what it means to be a team and how to win," Holtby said. "Maybe in the past we've had more skill or been better on paper or whatever. But this team, everyone knows their role and everyone wants to pitch in and everyone is comfortable with each other. I haven't been on a team like this where in any situation we're confident and confident in each other. We don't get down on each other."

The new additions brought growing pains, but they also didn't have the same "baggage," as veteran center Jay Beagle put it, as the longtime Capitals who had endured multiple playoff disappointments. But ultimately, it was on Washington's longest-tenured players to be the difference.

Ovechkin didn't shy away from the enormity of the moment. His own legacy has an asterisk next to it: one of the greatest players the NHL has ever seen but still not a champion.

"Of course, you have dreams, you have thoughts," Ovechkin said Tuesday. "Right now, you in this position, you just don't want to give up this opportunity."

Fans celebrated on F Street after watching Game 7 during a free viewing party at Capital One Arena. (PHOTO BY ANDRE CHUNG)

13
BAUER
WASHINGTON
capitals
OVECHKIN
8
BAUER
CCM

STANLEY CUP PLAYOFFS SECOND ROUND

CAPITALS 4, PENGUINS 2

Time to move on

BY ADAM KILGORE

Jakub Vrana, who celebrated with Alex Ovechkin after scoring the winning goal in Game 5, also had two assists. (PHOTO BY JONATHAN NEWTON)

In North American cities other than Washington, no matter how fortunate or cursed, no matter how rabid or indifferent, what happened here Monday night would have registered somewhere on the spectrum between mild celebration and contented shrug. There was no grand achievement, no banner earned, no trophy lifted. Washington Capitals players huddled and whooped at center ice, but they did not fling gloves and spray bubbly. It was, for those places allowed to have nice things, a triumph worthy of happiness, not history.

In Washington, though, Evgeny Kuznetsov's overtime, breakaway goal was an occasion worthy of marking the date and time: May 7, 2018, exactly 10 p.m. How does it feel, Washington? Teenagers in and around the Beltway have no clue, college kids from the DMV aren't old enough to know and everybody else can barely remember: Washington will root for a team vying for entry into the finals of one of the four major sports. It is an unremarkable sentence made remarkable for how long it has not been written.

Monday night at PPG Paints Arena, the Capitals snapped one of the strangest, cruelest and most improbable streaks in sports. They became the first Washington representative since 1998 to reach the conference finals in one of the four major North American sports, knocking out the defending Stanley Cup champion Pittsburgh Penguins with a 2-1 victory in Game 6 of the second round.

In its two-decade life span, the streak had left bitter notes on Presidents' Trophies, runaway National League East titles, blossoming first-overall draft picks and a phenom quarterback. It earned the label "D.C. Sports Curse," because karma provided order where logic could offer none. It turned regular season joyrides into postseason gut-punches. It got coaches fired, tainted players' reputations and made fans question their sanity. And now, it is dead.

"It's almost embarrassing it's taken this long for us to get past it," Capitals and Wizards owner Ted Leonsis said Monday night, smiling in the victorious visitors locker room.

Capitals goalie Braden Holtby, the hero of the series, insisted he did not know about Washington's staggering inability to reach a league's final four. But he could sense his professional home town's ache to advance further and how prior shortcomings had piled up. So far, he said, the Capitals have not done enough.

"As a group, we wanted to give our city more from a playoffs standpoint," Holtby said. "More doesn't mean a conference final. More means a Stanley Cup."

Elsewhere, the idea of making the conference finals does not infect a city's collective psyche. But other places don't have D.C.'s scars. Forty-four North American cities, including Las Vegas, which has only had one team for one season, had seen a conference finalist in one of the big four sports since Washington last saw one. It has become its own entity and made locals pick philosophical sides, such as whether to appreciate the constant contention or bemoan the annual letdown.

"The D.C. sports city thing is the biggest crock of crap in the entire world," Nationals first baseman Ryan Zimmerman said over the weekend. "If [people] don't like every one of their teams going to the playoffs every year, then they should go to a different city where no teams make playoffs. Where none of their teams are competitive every year. It's the biggest crock. Of course everybody wants their teams to win championships. Move to New England.

"I mean, I get it. Whatever. 'All the sports teams choke.' Every city besides one chokes every year. So what. Whatever. I know. It's fun for [media members]. It's a great city for being a sports fan. I think people should take the positives. Everyone's so negative nowadays. 'Oh, they didn't win the Stanley Cup.' Yeah, well they're a really good team every year that gives you guys something to go watch 80-something times a year that's going to be one of the better teams in the league. You could be a team that's terrible."

Monday night in San Diego, between the third period and overtime, Nationals General Manager Mike Rizzo reflected on the city's playoff disappointments while waiting for the game to come back on in the clubhouse. He said a victory would be "a good shot in the arm for the city," but he played down the psychic carry-over a Caps victory may have.

"I will say one thing: D.C. is in the playoffs in just about every sport, every year," Rizzo said. "How do you get over the hump? How do you win in the playoffs? You win in the playoffs by getting to the playoffs as many times as you can and giving yourselves as many chances as possible."

But what happens when the laws of probability forget one city? The Capitals, Nationals, Redskins and Wizards had played 71 seasons collectively without once advancing to the conference finals. The chance of any random team claiming one of four conference finals spots any random year in a 30-team league is 13.3 percent. The chance of betting on an outcome 71 times with a 13.3 percent chance of winning, and then losing every time, is 1 in 25,852.

But some of those teams were no random entrants; they were among the very best teams in their leagues. The Nationals led the National League in wins in a three-year span, and the Capitals won the Presidents' Trophy three times with Alex Ovechkin. Washington's four major sports teams played 13 games in which a victory would have advanced them to a conference final round. They lost all 13. The odds of losing 13 straight coins flips are 8,195 to 1.

Recent regular season success, even dominance, delivered a special kind of heartache. Anguish occurred with such overwhelming frequency and diabolical novelty that fans could be tempted to believe cosmic forces had aligned against them. The most joyous moments — Jayson Werth walking off, John Wall jumping on the scorer's table, 14-0 over the Seahawks — always led ultimately to more heartbreak.

Monday night reversed the script. The Capitals were undermanned, playing without injured Nicklas Backstrom and suspended Tom Wilson. The season was expected to be a regrouping under a coach, Barry Trotz, without a contract for next season. And yet there was Ovechkin, finding Kuznetsov breaking away at mid-ice. Now that they are finally in the third round, the Capitals have no interest in the city's milestone.

"The goal isn't to get past the second round," forward Jay Beagle said. "The goal is the Stanley Cup. That's always been the goal."

"I really want to win a Cup," Leonsis said. "While this feels good, we want to win a Cup."

After Kuznetsov scored and the Capitals spilled over the boards, out in San Diego several corners of the Nationals clubhouse celebrated along with the folks back home. Rizzo, eager for one more chance in one more October, pulled out his phone and sent a text message to a reporter. In other cities, it would have made no sense. In Washington, on this night, it was a rallying cry for a region.

It read: "What curse????"

GAME 1

PENGUINS 3, CAPITALS 2

A familiar villain leads a comeback

BY ISABELLE KHURSHUDYAN

In perhaps a fitting sequence for two superstars whose careers have become intertwined through repeated postseason battles, Pittsburgh's Sidney Crosby raised his arms in celebration as Washington's Alex Ovechkin smacked his stick against the glass in frustration.

Ovechkin's pass had led to the Capitals' first goal, and he had scored the second. Then Crosby played a part in the next three, the Penguins' top line outdueling the Capitals' in what was ultimately the difference in Game 1 of this second-round series. Pittsburgh's 3-2 win effectively stole the Capitals' home-ice advantage in the best-of-seven matchup.

What might make the loss sting more is that Washington had a two-goal lead in the third period and Pittsburgh was without one of its best players. For a second straight year these teams are meeting in the second round, and both times the Capitals have dropped the opener at home.

"One mistake, one bad bounce, and they're back in the game," Ovechkin said. "That's it, nothing you can say. It's over, so we have to focus on the next game."

On a two-on-one less than five minutes into the game, Ovechkin shanked a feed from defenseman Dmitry Orlov, missing a wide-open net and then dropping to both knees in disappointment. But with Washington clinging to a 1-0 lead as the third period started, Ovechkin barreled down the ice on another two-on-one, and this time he didn't miss, lifting the Capitals to a two-goal cushion just 28 seconds into the frame.

That marked Ovechkin's 100th career playoff point and his second of the night after he set up Evgeny Kuznetsov's first goal of the game, just 17 seconds after the puck dropped. But Washington had struggled to protect leads in its first-round series against Columbus, and that bad habit followed the Capitals into Game 1 against the

Penguins. Less than three minutes after Ovechkin's snap shot, Pittsburgh's Patric Hornqvist tipped a shot past goaltender Braden Holtby.

"We had areas where we played well, but we played into their strengths a little bit too much at times," Holtby said. "But we had our chances, too. It was one of those games that, with a lot of chances at both ends, you never know really what's going to happen. It's probably going to come down to a bounce or something like that."

That bounce was off Ovechkin's stick. On that Pittsburgh top line's next shift, a puck went off Ovechkin's blade and landed on Crosby's. He wristed a shot past Holtby to tie the game, and as Ovechkin skated around the back of the net, his frustration showed as he hit his stick against the glass.

The Penguins' top trio went back to the bench, and the next time they hopped over it, they scored once again. Crosby shot a puck off the wall, and Jake Guentzel deflected it, the puck changing direction as it fluttered under Holtby's armpit.

That capped a three-goal outburst on three consecutive shifts by the Penguins' first line in less than five minutes.

"It's pretty tough to talk about that right now, but overall I think we play pretty much an even game," Kuznetsov said. "They have good looks, we have good looks, but those three shifts changed the game, and it's again our third period. We have to be better over there."

Injuries to Penguins forwards Evgeni Malkin and Carl Hagelin presented the Capitals with an advantage before they even stepped on the ice. Malkin, the team's second-line center, was Pittsburgh's leading scorer during the season with 42 goals and 56 assists, and his absence gave Washington an edge up the middle. But the Capitals have blown similar opportunities against the Penguins in the past. In the series between the teams last year, Crosby missed Game 4 with a concussion, and Washington still lost. The year before that, top defenseman Kris Letang was suspended for a game in the series, and the Capitals didn't win that one either.

Washington got off to a good start with its first shift of the game. Ovechkin sprung Kuznetsov for a partial breakaway, and his quick release beat goaltender Matt Murray. But both teams seemed jittery for the rest of the frame. Several of the Capitals' passes were just a little off the mark, the puck landing in players' skates. But while his teammates played through some nervous energy, Holtby looked steady, protecting the 1-0 lead through 40 minutes.

He caught a break when Dominik Simon hit the post in the first period. He made a fantastic save when he slid across the crease to make a pad stop on Guentzel. He caught another break when Guentzel's shot on the first shift of the second period caromed off the cross bar. That luck turned in the third period, when Pittsburgh's top line was able to crowd Holtby and redirect pucks past him.

"It's one of those situations where you say it's 50-50 when there's two layers of screens," Holtby said. "You obviously want to shift into the deflection area, and I was shifting into both guys who were in front of me, not the high guys. Especially that last one, it kind of just hit him. It wasn't a planned thing. So I have to look at them again, but that's what happens when you have deflections."

The Penguins won the first two games in this building a year ago, putting the Capitals in a 2-0 hole before the series moved to Pittsburgh. A playoff format that pits division opponents against each other in the first two rounds has had these teams meet in the second round three years in a row now. The past two series were a pit stop for the Penguins en route to back-to-back Stanley Cup championships, while Washington, the league's best regular season team, was left devastated by how it again failed to reach the conference final.

With less than a minute left in Thursday night's Game 1, some fans started to head for the exits, the scene of Penguins celebrating on the Capitals' home ice all too familiar.

"You never want to go down, right? But sometimes, hockey gives you those opportunities to win the game, but you didn't," Kuznetsov said. "That's fine. It's just one game. We have to regroup and we have to stay positive because overall, we got some good looks."

APRIL 26 AT WASHINGTON

Pittsburgh	**0**	**0**	**3**	**3**
Washington	**1**	**0**	**1**	**2**

FIRST PERIOD
Scoring: 1, Washington, Kuznetsov 5 (Ovechkin, Wilson), 0:17.

SECOND PERIOD
Scoring: None.

THIRD PERIOD
Scoring: 2, Washington, Ovechkin 6 (Orlov, Wilson), 0:28. 3, Pittsburgh, Hornqvist 3 (Schultz, Guentzel), 2:59. 4, Pittsburgh, Crosby 7 (Guentzel, Hornqvist), 5:20. 5, Pittsburgh, Guentzel 7 (Crosby), 7:48.

SHOTS ON GOAL

Pittsburgh	9	8	8	25
Washington	6	10	18	34

Power-play opportunities: Pittsburgh 0 of 2; Washington 0 of 1.

Goalies: Pittsburgh, Murray 5-2 (34 shots-32 saves). Washington, Holtby 4-2 (25-22).

Devante Smith-Pelly, who had seven hits in Game 1, crashed into Penguins goaltender Matt Murray as he tried to score. (PHOTO BY TONI L. SANDYS)

GAME 2

CAPITALS 4, PENGUINS 1

It's wide open as Caps show some fight

BY ISABELLE KHURSHUDYAN

Alex Ovechkin scored the first goal of Game 2, and the Capitals didn't let up.
(PHOTO BY TONI L. SANDYS)

APRIL 29 AT WASHINGTON

Pittsburgh	**0**	**1**	**0**	**1**
Washington	**2**	**1**	**1**	**4**

FIRST PERIOD

Scoring: 1, Washington, Ovechkin 7, 1:26. 2, Washington, Vrana 1 (Eller, Holtby), 14:54 (pp).

SECOND PERIOD

Scoring: 3, Washington, Connolly 1 (Eller), 2:08. 4, Pittsburgh, Letang 2 (Schultz, Guentzel), 13:04.

THIRD PERIOD

Scoring: 5, Washington, Backstrom 3 (Wilson, Eller), 19:53.

SHOTS ON GOAL

Pittsburgh	10	16	7	33
Washington	20	6	6	32

Power-play opportunities: Pittsburgh 0 of 3; Washington 1 of 3.

Goalies: Pittsburgh, Murray 5-3 (31 shots-28 saves). Washington, Holtby 5-2 (33-32).

Amid the cheers, the whipping towels and dinging cowbells at Capital One Arena, there was also an exhale. Washington Capitals forward Brett Connolly scored on a partial breakaway, and the sight of the puck in the net and a red goal light brought both joy and relief. Washington wouldn't be squandering a two-goal lead, because the team now was up three.

The Capitals ultimately won by that margin, 4-1, and with the next two games in Pittsburgh, Washington has tied the second-round Stanley Cup playoff series against the Penguins at one game apiece, in large part thanks to goaltender Braden Holtby's 32 saves and some good fortune with video reviews. Most importantly, the Capitals continued to build on their lead rather than cling to it.

"You can see what happen last game when we get the lead 2-0, and they come back and win the game," captain Alex Ovechkin said. "They're experienced team.

"They're not going to give up and they're not going to give easy play for us. We have to earn it. Today I think we play a solid game. Everybody was in, and we get the result."

After 20 minutes, the Capitals found themselves in a familiar, uneasy position. For the second straight game, Washington was up 2-0, but the team had squandered that kind of cushion three times in its previous seven playoff games, including Game 1 against the Penguins.

The postseason had been miserable for Connolly a year ago. He played in just seven games, a healthy scratch for the other six as Washington opted to play seven defensemen with 11 forwards. When Connolly did play, his ice time was limited. This playoff run has taken an opposite arc. He has gotten more responsibility with a promotion to the third line. He had been unable to convert on numerous chances in past games, but with the partial breakaway in the second period Sunday he didn't miss, and his wrist shot lifted the Capitals to a 3-0 lead 2:08 into the second period.

"Even when we go up three, you've got to keep playing against this team because they can hurt you in a lot of different ways," Connolly said.

Pittsburgh's Kris Letang scored roughly 11 minutes later with a point shot while Holtby had two layers of screens in front of him. The Penguins seemed to score again midway through the third period, when Patric Hornqvist jammed in a wraparound attempt by Sidney Crosby. But the officials didn't call it a goal on the ice, and a long video review followed. Holtby had stopped the puck with his pad, but it was unclear whether it had managed to cross the goal line anyway. The video review didn't provide a definitive replay, so the Penguins didn't receive the tally, another break for Washington in a game of them.

"Sometimes it goes your way, sometimes not," center Nicklas Backstrom said. "We got lucky there."

The Capitals had caught one break before the game even started. With Penguins center Evgeni Malkin and winger Carl Hagelin both out with injuries in Game 1, Washington didn't take advantage of the opportunity, a theme in past postseason series between the teams. A year ago, the Capitals lost the game Crosby missed with a concussion. The year before that, top defenseman Letang was suspended for a game, and the Capitals didn't win then, either.

Malkin was Pittsburgh's leading scorer this season with 42 goals and 56 assists in 78 games, and Washington got another opportunity when Malkin's undisclosed lower-body injury kept him out of Game 2, too. With Crosby and Malkin on the team, the Penguins have never lost a playoff series in which they took a two-games-to-none lead.

"Obviously, he's a top player. There's no question about it," Capitals Coach Barry Trotz said before the game. "But at the same time, it doesn't really matter. We've just got to win the game."

Washington again got the strong start it wanted; the team has scored first in all but one of its eight playoff games. Less than two minutes into the game, Capitals center Evgeny Kuznetsov and Hornqvist raced for a puck that had slid into Pittsburgh's zone. Hornqvist got his stick on it, but he inadvertently passed it to Ovechkin, who quickly shot it past Matt Murray's glove for the first goal of the game. That was Ovechkin's second goal in as many games and his third point.

Then, with five seconds left in a power play, rookie Jakub Vrana maneuvered through three Pittsburgh sticks to get to the front of the net and beat Murray glove side. That seemed like a target for Washington; Connolly's goal also was to Murray's glove side. The Penguins challenged for goaltender interference because Connolly's stick had made contact with Murray's leg before Vrana's goal, but the league determined that Connolly's actions didn't impair Murray from making the save, so the goal stood.

"Honestly, I didn't really even know that I did that," Connolly said. "I was shocked. It's just a quick reaction. You're kind of being intense, but it was way before. ... We deserved that break. We've been playing so well. We deserved a break tonight."

And then the Capitals made their own break, with Connolly getting the all-important third goal, insurance the series would be tied.

Pittsburgh was denied a goal when a video review provided no definitive evidence that a puck under Braden Holtby crossed the line. (PHOTO BY JONATHAN NEWTON)

MURRAY

GAME 3

CAPITALS 4, PENGUINS 3

Ovechkin's late goal gives Caps series lead

BY ISABELLE KHURSHUDYAN

Alex Ovechkin beat Pittsburgh netminder Matt Murray for the decisive goal with just 1:07 remaining in Game 3. The score came after a pass from Nicklas Backstrom. (PHOTO BY TONI L. SANDYS)

MAY 1 AT PITTSBURGH

Washington	**0**	**2**	**2**	**4**
Pittsburgh	**0**	**3**	**0**	**3**

FIRST PERIOD
Scoring: None.

SECOND PERIOD
Scoring: 1, Washington, Carlson 2 (Backstrom, Ovechkin), 0:48 (pp). 2, Pittsburgh, Guentzel 8 (Crosby, Schultz), 4:33. 3, Pittsburgh, Hornqvist 4 (Kessel, Malkin), 6:49 (pp). 4, Washington, Stephenson 2 (Backstrom, Oshie), 11:04. 5, Pittsburgh, Crosby 8 (Letang, Guentzel), 16:27.

THIRD PERIOD
Scoring: 6, Washington, Niskanen 1 (Orlov, Wilson), 5:06. 7, Washington, Ovechkin 8 (Backstrom), 18:53.

SHOTS ON GOAL

Washington	7	5	10	22
Pittsburgh	9	10	3	22

Power-play opportunities:
Washington 1 of 4; Pittsburgh 1 of 4

Goalies: Washington, Holtby 6-2 (22 shots-19 saves). Pittsburgh, Murray 5-4 (22-18).

The shift started disastrously for the Washington Capitals. With less than two minutes left in the third period, the Pittsburgh Penguins circled in front of Capitals goaltender Braden Holtby, appearing to have a power play without the actual man advantage. Washington center Nicklas Backstrom finally got the puck out, and he and captain Alex Ovechkin skated together down the ice.

Backstrom had the freshest legs on the ice after jumping on for Evgeny Kuznetsov just 20 seconds earlier. Everyone else was exhausted, and the two-on-one seemed to unfold in slow motion. “Probably the first time in my career that I looked fast,” Backstrom said with a smirk.

The Penguins have tortured Backstrom and Ovechkin, Washington’s longest-tenured players, in playoffs past. On Tuesday night, Backstrom passed to Ovechkin on the two-on-one, and after Ovechkin hit the post with the first shot he batted in the rebound with just 1:07 remaining, lifting the Capitals to a 4-3 win and a 2-1 lead in the best-of-seven second-round series. Washington is 4-0 on the road in these Stanley Cup playoffs.

“I mean, if you want to be successful in the playoffs you have got to win on the road, and especially because they won the first game, too,” Backstrom said. “It’s nicer to be up 2-1 than being down 2-1. We’re just excited for the next game.”

The Capitals scored three of their goals in Game 2 on Pittsburgh goaltender Matt Murray’s glove side, perhaps identifying a weakness. With the Penguins leading by one through 40 minutes Tuesday, it was Murray’s glove side that enabled Washington to draw even. Capitals defenseman Matt Niskanen’s shot from the point seemed to be going wide until Murray tipped it with his glove, deflecting it into his own net 5:06 into the third period.

The game seemed to be heading to overtime until Ovechkin’s late goal stunned the crowd of yellow-clad fans at PPG Paints Arena. “I hit the post, and it’s a good thing I didn’t raise my arms up,” Ovechkin said. “I finished up the play and got lucky.”

“Those two are dynamic together,” Capitals Coach Barry Trotz said of Ovechkin and Backstrom.

Both of Washington’s special-teams units have improved in the postseason. A power play with Ovechkin in the left faceoff circle is always dangerous, and the Capitals have scored at least one man-advantage goal in all but one of their nine playoff games. But it has been the penalty kill that has often been the difference for Washington. Entering Tuesday’s game, the team hadn’t allowed a power-play goal since Game 2 against Columbus in the first round, and in Game 3 against Pittsburgh, the Capitals’ shorthanded unit allowed Washington to settle in after a jumpy start.

Brett Connolly and T.J. Oshie were both called for offensive-zone infractions within the first 10 minutes, but the Capitals killed their 23rd and 24th straight penalties. Washington’s penalty kill was ranked 15th during the regular season at 80.2 percent, and that had jumped to 86.3 percent through the Capitals’ first eight playoff games.

Washington’s power play netted the first goal Tuesday with John Carlson’s point shot 48 seconds into the second period, but the Penguins answered less than four minutes later when Jake Guentzel tipped a Justin Schultz shot past Holtby. Then, on Pittsburgh’s third power play, Washington’s penalty kill finally broke. Patric Hornqvist outmuscled Dmitry Orlov in front, swatting in a rebound from Evgeni Malkin to give Pittsburgh a 2-1 lead 6:49 into the second period.

The Penguins’ lineup got a boost with the return of Malkin, who had missed the first two games of the series with an apparent leg injury. Malkin, who led Pittsburgh in scoring this season, added even more firepower to the team’s power play, and he also allowed Penguins Coach Mike Sullivan to spread his top scorers across multiple lines, making Pittsburgh deeper and harder to match up against. Phil Kessel, who scored 34 goals this season, was on a third line, while Derick Brassard (21 goals) centered the fourth line. Sullivan also made a concerted effort to get captain Sidney Crosby away from Washington’s top defensive pairing of Niskanen and Orlov.

But after Capitals winger Chandler Stephenson tied the game with a snap shot in

Tom Wilson fell into the Washington bench after his hit on Zach Aston-Reese that left the Pittsburgh rookie with a concussion and a broken jaw. (PHOTO BY TONI L. SANDYS)

front, the teams went to four-on-four for two minutes 15:55 into what was an eventful second period. Washington had Orlov and Niskanen on the ice against the Penguins' dynamic duo of Guentzel and Crosby. Guentzel turned Orlov inside-out, stickhandling around him and pushing the puck through his legs before setting up Crosby's go-ahead goal. Pittsburgh took that 3-2 lead to the second intermission.

These teams have a long rivalry with each other, but tensions seemed especially high before the game after a controversial collision between Pittsburgh's Brian Dumoulin and Washington's Tom Wilson in Game 2. Dumoulin was knocked out for the rest of the game after Wilson made contact with his head in the second period, but the NHL deemed the contact "unavoidable" because of how Dumoulin changed his position before impact with Wilson.

Wilson was booed whenever he touched the puck Tuesday night, and the fans' displeasure with him grew more pronounced after his hit on Penguins forward Zach Aston-Reese in the second period caused Aston-Reese to leave the ice. There was no penalty on the play, but it will inevitably be scrutinized to see if Wilson hit Aston-Reese's shoulder or head first, the latter potentially leading to supplemental discipline. Aston-Reese suffered a concussion and a broken jaw on the hit, Sullivan said.

But as the game grew nastier and the crowd turned on Washington even more, the Capitals seemed to settle in, apparently comfortable with the hostility.

"It was a game we had to work right to the end for," Holtby said. "That was our goal coming in. I thought we played really well in a lot of areas. They were forcing us to be real patient and wait for our chances, and it was a real tough game for both teams. We accomplished what we wanted to, and now we enjoy it for a couple minutes and refocus and focus on Game 4."

GAME 4

PENGUINS 3, CAPITALS 1

Momentum lost with Wilson out

BY ISABELLE KHURSHUDYAN

It was ironic that a penalty for too many men on the ice sealed the loss for the Capitals, preventing Washington from getting a man-advantage when it pulled goaltender Braden Holtby. The Capitals seemed shorthanded for the entire contest.

The Pittsburgh Penguins' 3-1 win Thursday night tied the best-of-seven series at 2-2, with two of the next three games in Washington. Though the Capitals said the absence of suspended top-line right wing Tom Wilson would motivate them, it also was evident how much he was missed, especially as captain Alex Ovechkin was held without a shot on goal in a playoff game for just the third time in his career.

"Trust me, Ovi will get his shots," Capitals Coach Barry Trotz said.

"If you play Pittsburgh, you're not going to win if you score one goal," center Nicklas Backstrom said. "You need more."

The Capitals entered the game more than a little peeved. The team was unhappy with the NHL Department of Player Safety's decision to suspend Wilson for three games because of an illegal check to the head of Pittsburgh's Zach Aston-Reese, who suffered a broken jaw and a concussion.

T.J. Oshie passionately defended Wilson on Thursday morning and called a three-game suspension "very extreme." Oshie said the rest of the team would have to make up for the loss of Wilson's physicality, and the Capitals had 43 hits to the Penguins' 25. Oshie led the way with eight.

"Any arrogance that we might have had from our last couple of victories has been squashed from the fact that we're losing Tom, that he's been taken away from us for a couple games here," Oshie said before the game. "We're fired up to play, and we want to win the game for him."

But Wilson's absence was a hit to a Washington forward corps already missing winger Andre Burakovsky, who recently had surgery for an undisclosed upper-body injury. Devante Smith-Pelly moved into Wilson's right wing spot on the top line with Ovechkin and Evgeny Kuznetsov.

That line looked disjointed throughout the game, and Ovechkin, who has eight goals this postseason, never got a shot on goal, held without so much as an attempt for the first 40 minutes. The trio were on the ice when Pittsburgh's Jake Guentzel punched in a rebound for the first goal 9:21 into the second period.

"Devo did a really good job filling in," Trotz said of Smith-Pelly. "Obviously, Tom is a unique player. But I thought that line was going head-to-head pretty well. There wasn't much space out there on both sides."

The Penguins have been hurting for secondary scoring — every Pittsburgh goal this series has come with captain Sidney Crosby on the ice — but Guentzel has shined. His 10 goals and 11 assists lead all players in postseason scoring. He added an empty-netter in the last minute of the game, after the too-many-men penalty to Washington. That was the Penguins' 24th and final shot. The Capitals managed just 21, with both teams unable to get much going offensively.

Oshie tied the game on Washington's second power play, one-timing a slick feed from Backstrom. But then it was Oshie who helped deliver the lead back to the Penguins.

He was called for interference on defenseman Brian Dumoulin, and Pittsburgh took advantage of the power play. Evgeni Malkin dived for a rebound, knocking the puck in the direction of Holtby's outstretched blocker. Just as in Game 2, there was a review to see whether the puck had indeed crossed the goal line, and this time the goal counted for the Penguins.

"I shot us in the foot there with that penalty," Oshie said. "I was trying to make a smart play by taking away their [defenseman's] stick, and it ended up being a dumb play by clipping his skate there. That was kind of the turning point in the game, when they got that goal there when I was in the box. So I've got to be a little smarter than that."

Trotz then challenged for goaltender interference, and the league's decision was swift there, too, again in favor of Pittsburgh.

"You can complain about this or complain about that or wonder about this or whatever," defenseman Matt Niskanen said. "You just keep playing the game really hard and keep believing. I think we're building a belief that we can beat these guys. We know we're going to have to play really well, but it's possible. We think we can do it. We've just got to play really well."

MAY 3 AT PITTSBURGH

Washington	**0**	**1**	**0**	**1**
Pittsburgh	**0**	**2**	**1**	**3**

FIRST PERIOD

Scoring: None.

SECOND PERIOD

Scoring: 1, Pittsburgh, Guentzel 9 (Crosby, Simon), 9:21. 2, Washington, Oshie 4 (Backstrom, Kuznetsov), 12:55 (pp). 3, Pittsburgh, Malkin 4 (Hornqvist, Kessel), 17:31 (pp).

THIRD PERIOD

Scoring: 4, Pittsburgh, Guentzel 10, 19:02 (pp).

SHOTS ON GOAL

Washington	7	11	3	21
Pittsburgh	9	8	7	24

Power-play opportunities: Washington 1 of 3; Pittsburgh 2 of 4.

Goalies: Washington, Holtby 6-3 (23 shots-21 saves). Pittsburgh, Murray 6-4 (21-20).

Crosby again has a hand in everything as Penguins knot series

As the final moments of an ugly and sometimes grisly Game 4 arrived and the Washington Capitals made their final push to erase a one-goal deficit, Pittsburgh Penguins captain Sidney Crosby made one of the most aesthetically pleasing plays of the night. Crosby, of course, made it look routine.

He was near the side boards as the puck was flung high into the air. He glided toward it and snatched it out of the air as oncoming traffic barreled his way — Capitals captain Alex Ovechkin had his rival in his crosshairs — but Crosby simply tossed the puck to the ice, glided past Ovechkin and passed the puck across center ice to teammate Jake Guentzel.

It was only appropriate that Crosby was involved: He has been on the ice for all 10 of Pittsburgh's goals in this series, helping shepherd yet another breakout postseason performance by Guentzel and anchoring a Pittsburgh lineup that has dealt with attrition and a lack of secondary scoring against the Capitals.

"I think you have confidence in whoever you play with [that] they're going to play their role and do what they do and contribute in any way that they need to," said Crosby, who essentially deflected any praise.

— Roman Stubbs

John Carlson, who had three of Washington's 43 hits, collided with Chad Ruhwedel. (PHOTO BY TONI L. SANDYS)

WASHINGTON
Capitals
77
CCM

GAME 5

CAPITALS 6, PENGUINS 3

Uncharted territory as Caps find hope

BY ISABELLE KHURSHUDYAN

T.J. Oshie, who assisted on a first-period goal, gave Washington insurance with his third-period empty-net score. (PHOTO BY JOHN MCDONNELL)

MAY 5 AT WASHINGTON

Pittsburgh	1	2	0	3
Washington	2	0	4	6

FIRST PERIOD

Scoring: 1, Pittsburgh, Oleksiak 1 (Sheary, Brassard), 2:23. 2, Washington, Carlson 3 (Kuznetsov, Oshie), 18:22 (pp). 3, Washington, Connolly 2 (Eller, Vrana), 18:55.

SECOND PERIOD

Scoring: 4, Pittsburgh, Crosby 9 (Schultz, Kessel), 4:43 (pp). 5, Pittsburgh, Hornqvist 5 (Kessel, Malkin), 7:45 (pp).

THIRD PERIOD

Scoring: 6, Washington, Kuznetsov 6 (Niskanen, Vrana), 0:52. 7, Washington, Vrana 2 (Ovechkin, Kuznetsov), 15:22. 8, Washington, Oshie 5, 18:29 (en). 9, Washington, Eller 3 (Beagle), 19:54 (en).

SHOTS ON GOAL

Pittsburgh	13	18	8	39
Washington	13	5	14	32

Power-play opportunities: Pittsburgh 2 of 5; Washington 1 of 3.

Goalies: Pittsburgh, Murray 6-4 (30 shots-26 saves). Washington, Holtby 6-3 (39-36).

The Washington Capitals' game-saving — and maybe playoff-saving — goal came from a 22-year-old rookie unburdened by the organization's tortured postseason history. Jakub Vrana was 2 years old the last time the Capitals got past the second round. He was a scratch in the first round of this postseason. He barely saw the ice at the start of this series. He was a hero Saturday night.

In a tied third period, Vrana followed Alex Ovechkin down the ice, and after Ovechkin skated to the right of Pittsburgh Penguins goaltender Matt Murray to pull him out of position, Ovechkin lightly put a pass into the slot for Vrana, who tapped the puck into a wide-open net as if it was no big deal. He tried to keep that composure as he stood in front of a line of reporters in the locker room after the game, but then he showed the youth and exuberance that has made him a crucial piece of this Capitals team.

"Obviously, it feels really [expletive] good," Vrana said quickly as he took a deep breath.

That goal stood as the game-winner in Washington's 6-3 victory over the Penguins. T.J. Oshie and Lars Eller added late empty-net goals to secure the result, and the Capitals are now one win away from advancing to the conference finals for a first time in 20 years. Saturday's victory came because of a key midgame adjustment from Coach Barry Trotz, who promoted Vrana to the top line with Ovechkin and center Evgeny Kuznetsov.

"I think the playoffs build a lot of character," Trotz said. "They build confidence, and Jake has stayed with it. He's had stretches this year where he's gone 21 games without even a goal on our second line, playing substantial minutes. For a young guy to battle through that and navigate a young career, sometimes you could get a little frustrated. I think we've really done a really good job of managing him and getting him to understand that there's so many things that you can contribute if you're not just scoring.

"I think he's learned that, he's settled in, and he's a contributing player now."

Just 52 seconds into the third period, Kuznetsov got to flap his wings. He collected a pass from Vrana in the neutral zone, and with Pittsburgh's top defensive pairing caught out of position, Kuznetsov got a breakaway, beating Murray with a backhand shot through his legs. Then, in a celebration not seen since the Capitals played the Penguins last postseason, Kuznetsov lifted one leg and imitated a bird as he fanned his arms up and down.

But just as Washington started to play its best hockey of the game in the third period, center Nicklas Backstrom left the bench and went to the locker room with an "upper-body" injury. Something seemed off with him all game, as center Chandler Stephenson took the faceoffs for Backstrom. The Capitals are already down two regular top-six forwards with Andre Burakovsky injured and Tom Wilson suspended for one more game, so an injury to Backstrom could be devastating.

But even playing down a forward, the Capitals showed a resiliency not seen in past postseasons. It started with goaltender Braden Holtby, who had made 28 saves through two periods. He saved a point-blank shot by defenseman Brian Dumoulin, and that led to Vrana and Ovechkin's rush up the ice for the game-winning goal.

Trotz had seemed hesitant to trust Vrana before this game. He can be a defensive liability, especially against Pittsburgh's superstar forward corps, but he also has dynamic speed and offensive upside the Capitals haven't had in past series against the Penguins.

"Obviously it means a lot when the coach trusts you for a player," Vrana said. "You just get confidence. It's a big responsibility. You've just got to make sure you go out there and get those little details right."

Both Trotz and Ovechkin acknowledged that the top line needed to be better after it struggled in Game 4, just the third playoff game in Ovechkin's career in which he didn't record a single shot on goal. He rectified that on the first shift Saturday, putting the first puck on net in the game with a wrist shot 15 feet in front of the net. Murray saved it, and momentum seemed to favor the Penguins when Conor Sheary screened Holtby as defenseman Jamie Oleksiak's point shot scored 2:23 into the game.

Rookie Jakub Vrana, who was promoted to the No. 1 line with Alex Ovechkin and Evgeny Kuznetsov midgame, scored the go-ahead goal in the third period. (PHOTO BY JONATHAN NEWTON)

Ovechkin finished with three shots on goal by the end of the first period, and it was just his presence that allowed the Capitals to tie the score. Pittsburgh's Dominik Simon was whistled for tripping in the offensive zone, and with the Penguins' penalty kill shading Ovechkin, defenseman John Carlson had plenty of room as he ripped a shot past Murray's glove.

Thirty-three seconds after his goal, Washington took the lead. Vrana won a puck battle along the wall and set up Brett Connolly in the high slot. The puck went off Patric Hornqvist's hand before fluttering through Murray's legs.

But Washington's penalty kill seemed to miss Wilson, suspended for three games after an illegal check to the head in Game 3 of the series, and as the Capitals took damaging penalties — hooking and slashing minors by Ovechkin and two tripping infractions by Devante Smith-Pelly — the Penguins got four straight man-advantage opportunities. They scored on two of them to take a 3-2 lead into the second intermission, and the Capitals were fortunate to be down by just a goal through 40 minutes. Pittsburgh had outshot Washington 18-5 in the second period.

The Capitals seemed mellow after their loss in Game 4, and Trotz had opted against making any changes to his lineup. But as the Capitals found themselves a period away from being pushed to the brink of elimination, Trotz started to make adjustments. He then moved Vrana to the first line with Ovechkin and Kuznetsov.

Less than a minute into the third period, Vrana's pass sprung Kuznetsov for a breakaway, the game-tying goal. He then delivered the game-winning one shortly after.

"There's a lot of belief in this room," Oshie said. "We know the history. We know what's happened to us in the past. But right now, we have a lot of belief and a lot of trust in each other."

87
KEMPNY
6
HOLTBY
70
CCM

GAME 6

CAPITALS 2, PENGUINS 1

Caps, and D.C., break through to semifinals

BY BARRY SVRLUGA

Pittsburgh's Sidney Crosby, left, and Brian Dumoulin skated away as Washington players celebrated Evgeny Kuznetsov's breakaway goal in overtime. The Capitals advanced to the Eastern Conference finals for the first time since 1998. (PHOTO BY TONI L. SANDYS)

MAY 7 AT PITTSBURGH

Washington	**0**	**1**	**0**	**1**	**2**
Pittsburgh	**0**	**1**	**0**	**0**	**1**

FIRST PERIOD
Scoring: None.

SECOND PERIOD
Scoring: 1, Washington, Chiasson 1 (Beagle, Walker), 2:13. 2, Pittsburgh, Letang 3 (Dumoulin, Crosby), 11:52.

THIRD PERIOD
Scoring: None.

OVERTIME
Scoring: 3, Washington, Kuznetsov 7 (Ovechkin, Orlov), 5:27.

SHOTS ON GOAL

Washington	7	8	9	6	30
Pittsburgh	6	9	5	2	22

Power-play opportunities:
Washington 0 of 1; Pittsburgh 0 of 1.

Goalies: Washington, Holtby 8-3 (22 shots-21 saves). Pittsburgh, Murray 6-6 (30-28).

It was one play in one moment as 10 p.m. approached on a Monday night in May, but when the puck landed on Evgeny Kuznetsov's stick and he took a powerful stride to the goal, decades rode with him. Tell us the teams in our town aren't intertwined with their fates. Point out that one version of the Washington Capitals has nothing to do with those that came before it.

"I never focus on the history," Kuznetsov said.

And yet there it was, on his stick blade. So much history. For the Capitals and the Pittsburgh Penguins, a nemesis if there ever was one. For the man who found Kuznetsov open in the middle of the ice, Alex Ovechkin. For Washington as a sports town, questioning belief and commitment and whether hope was sustainable — or even worth it.

Pretend those elements weren't intertwined at that moment. If they hadn't been, maybe Ovechkin's thoughts — which he relayed on a live NBC Sports Network interview almost immediately afterward — would have been something other than this: "Please score. Please @$#%&! score."

Imagine that.

Let's acknowledge, to the rest of the country, that the Capitals' 2-1 victory Monday night at PPG Paints Arena won them no banner or trophy. It was a hard-earned, overtime victory in the sixth game of their second-round playoff series. In some cities — Pittsburgh included — winning a second-round series might seem like a necessary step, not a milestone.

For Washington, though? The ignominious stats just grew year after year, to the point that the Nationals were asked about the Capitals, and the Capitals were asked about the Wizards, and the Redskins were — well, gee whiz. For two decades, since the Capitals made their only appearance in the Stanley Cup finals, no D.C. team in the four major professional North American sports stayed alive until just four teams remained. We had to think: Were they tied together in misery?

Maybe that's a lame story line. But it existed. It breathed and slept and woke and walked and lived among us. Ovechkin first appeared in a Capitals sweater — one of those blue-and-black-and-gold relics — back in the fall of 2005. Never had the greatest goal-scorer of his generation made it past the second round.

"It's always thrown in your face everywhere you turn," said Capitals Coach Barry Trotz, who shared that same distinction. "I know it's thrown in Ovi's face everywhere he turns."

Now, finally, he can throw it back.

"Alex's place in history is pretty set," Capitals owner Ted Leonsis said in the locker room afterward. In a way, that's true, because you can't take away from his three Hart Trophies as the NHL's MVP, and you can't take away his seven times leading the league in goals, and you can't take away the 607 regular season goals — or the fact that he essentially reshaped hockey in Washington.

But what evaporated Monday night was the big "but" people always brought with Ovechkin. Now, there will still be people who say — if this run ends in the Eastern Conference finals against the Tampa Bay Lightning — that Ovechkin was good but not great, that he still hasn't won a Stanley Cup.

Fine. But when he looked up ice in overtime and saw Kuznetsov, he had the opportunity to beat the Penguins, to say, for the first time in four second-round chances, that he got past Sidney Crosby. It might not mean much to people in other cities. It means a heck of a lot to people in Washington. "He threw the big pass — not the shot — to win it," Leonsis said. "I thought that was a moment that says where he's arrived as a player. I think he's a player and a captain who just wants to win."

These Capitals have been saddened by all the failings in the past, but they have also been hardened by them.

"They probably needed to go through some of this," Trotz said. "What I see is: There's growth." And so, when the Capitals showed up Monday, and it was apparent that Backstrom — a key to just about everything they do — wouldn't be able to go because of what appears to be a hand injury, they didn't buckle. They bucked up.

There was no Tom Wilson, serving the last of his three-game suspension. There was no Andre Burakovsky, who never appeared in the series because of an injury.

But there was also a lack of something else, something that has followed this franchise for so long. There was no doubt.

"The great thing about this all day," Trotz said, "is I knew we were going to win."

It's an odd thing to say, but there's some reason there, too. With such a thin lineup, some of the tried and tired themes about what the Capitals do in these situations — that they choke, that they gag, that they find ways to lose — were kind of eliminated. The puck hadn't yet dropped, and the favorite in this one 60-minute game was clearly established. It was Pittsburgh. The Capitals could only hope to win one in a way they never could have a decade or, maybe, even a year ago. They had to put the pestle to the mortar and grind.

And so when they forced overtime, it was the crowd at PPG Paints Arena that was on edge. Not the Caps. Which brings us back to the history that rushed up from behind and informed the entire night. As Ovechkin said afterward, "Nobody expect we going to be in this position before this season," and he's right. The Capitals' time was last year, when they posted the best record in the league for the second straight season, when they went all-in at the trade deadline to win a Cup.

When they didn't, they had to assess why. So it's worth listening to Brian MacLellan, the general manager, in a frank assessment in the days before the season even began. "We got to get to that point, when you feel that point of pressure from the whole history of it, the building, everything — that you overcome it," MacLellan said. "Somebody steps up."

So there was Ovechkin in overtime, looking up ice. There was the pass to Kuznetsov, and the rush in on the net. There was Pittsburgh goaltender Matt Murray. And there was the shot. You can say it was one play in one hockey game on one night in May. But for this town and this team, decades of drama and disappointment were wrapped up right there. Kuznetsov buried them all.

Evgeny Kuznetsov buried a lot of Washington disappointment when he deposited his overtime goal past Pittsburgh's Matt Murray. (PHOTO BY JONATHAN NEWTON)

OVECHKIN
8
8
SAP
OFFICIAL
APP
Jägermeister
CCM
CCM
CCM

STANLEY CUP PLAYOFFS FIRST ROUND

CAPITALS 4, BLUE JACKETS 2

All the way back

BY BARRY SVRLUGA

Alex Ovechkin scored five goals in six games against Columbus to set up a clash with nemesis Pittsburgh. (PHOTO BY TONI L. SANDYS)

We can debate whether it's fair — and it's probably not — but it doesn't alter the reality of the situation. Whatever the Washington Capitals' fate, in this or any postseason for the past dozen years, it is tied to the legacy and reputation of one Alex Ovechkin.

For a night and a series, let's allow the issue to rest. This Capitals' run in the Stanley Cup playoffs staved off disappointment, for now, in part because Alex Ovechkin is on this team. These Capitals — again, they are Ovechkin's Capitals until they aren't — are alive because when he had a chance to push Washington to the second round, he did. He scored the goal that put the Capitals ahead. He scored the trademark power-play marker that gave them a cushion. He was a force.

What the Capitals' 6-3 victory over the Columbus Blue Jackets in Game 6 of their first-round Stanley Cup playoff series gave the hockey world is what the hockey world wants, another matchup between Ovechkin's Capitals and their chief nemesis, Sidney Crosby's Pittsburgh Penguins. Nationally, that matchup may set up for punchlines at the Capitals' expense, because they have met three times before and the results have been Penguins in seven, Penguins in six and Penguins in seven — the last two in each of the last two years, perhaps leaving the deepest, darkest scars on both Ovechkin and a Caps fan base that so desperately wants its captain and hero to break through that wall.

So here, there's another chance. Ovechkin, fresh off a series in which he had eight points in six games — and a game in which he scored the 50th and 51st playoff goals of his career — is ready.

"I said it before: I can't wait," Ovechkin said Monday night. "It's a huge opportunity for us to take a step forward. Obviously, it's the Stanley Cup champion back-to-back. They know how to play. They know how to handle the pressure."

Forget the line about how the Caps don't know those things. Maybe it will come into play. Maybe not. But save it. It's not for now. Because now is an opportunity. For the Capitals. And for Ovechkin. "We look to 'O' to set an example," forward T.J. Oshie said.

The example, too, isn't so much that unstoppable blast from the left circle, the one that makes the jump to hyperspace before the Empire is even aware it has been launched. That's how Ovechkin's second goal came Monday night, the one that put Washington up 3-1. But the first one, the rebound off a Brooks Orpik shot from the point. That's the goal that Ovechkin scored again this season, the goal in which he puts his big rig of a body in front of the net, the goal that makes a difference in playoff games.

"Just adding layers to his game," Coach Barry Trotz said.

This season, in a way, has been about adding those layers, or re-adding layers he once had but abandoned. That, in turn, allowed Ovechkin to enhance — and elongate — his legacy.

When last year ended in the same, miserable way it always seems to end — a brutal home loss in the playoffs, this one in the seventh game of the second round, again to hated Pittsburgh — I laid a lot of the loss at Ovechkin's feet. It wasn't just that game or that series, but the fact that he is the common thread through all the pain over almost a decade.

The truth is, the Caps were outplayed in net in that series; Marc-Andre Fleury, who would be the Penguins' backup by the time they won the Cup, was better than Braden Holtby.

But in those playoffs, Trotz dropped Ovechkin from his customary, nearly permanent, spot on the first line down to the third. Ovechkin was on the ice for both of the Penguins' Game 7 goals. And as the offseason turned into 2017-18, Capitals General Manager Brian MacLellan was frank about what his star needed to do not just to maintain his customary level of production but to remain relevant in a league that is skewing younger: Ovi, MacLellan said, had to improve his speed and return to being a force at even strength, not just the guy who sets up in his Barcalounger on the power play, content to launch missiles and rack up numbers there.

It was an alarming way to speak about the player who is arguably the most important in the history of the franchise. But none of it was exaggerated. It was a simple, honest, harsh assessment of one of the sport's pillars as he turned 32, as he headed toward what seemed like it might be the twilight of his career. But it was all true.

So how did Ovechkin respond? With a hat trick on opening night, then four goals in the second game of the year. Further flipping off his critics, six of those goals came at even strength. And by the end of the year, what did he have but a league-best 49 goals? The only player to score more than Ovechkin's 32 at even strength: Edmonton Oilers wunderkind Connor McDavid.

And yet through it all, in the run to a third straight Metropolitan Division title that would not have happened had Ovechkin not been a force, he returned to a theme he has hit on with increasing frequency as the years move on. He brought it up again Monday night.

"It's all about team," Ovechkin said.

That's an easy thing to say, a tougher thing to display. And yet there was Ovechkin, late in the third with the Capitals nursing a two-goal lead, the time in a playoff game when each second seems to take five to click off the clock. In that time when games are decided, Ovechkin sold out to block a shot.

"That gets the boys going on the bench when you see him doing stuff like that," Oshie said.

"That's full commitment," Trotz said. "... That's where you get your street cred with your teammates. It's those details, those necessary details, that allow you to win."

By this point, at the end of his 13th NHL season, should Ovechkin need to earn street cred with his teammates? Put that discussion down. The Penguins are on the way to Washington. Ovechkin's Capitals have never pushed through this team, pushed through this round, to get to the Eastern Conference finals. He knows it. We all know it.

"We've been struggling in the second round, and we just have to believe in each other," he said. "Don't look what's happened in previous years. It's this year. It's new season. It's new series."

Maybe a new result. When the final horn sounded Monday, Ovechkin led the Capitals over the boards to greet Holtby. This wasn't a mob scene. It was a business-like handshake on what was, at its most basic, a business trip.

We have no idea what the rest of these playoffs will deliver. The mere existence of them brings the possibility of more pain. But we know the next week and a half brings Washington vs. Pittsburgh, one more time. And if Alex Ovechkin wasn't around, it's doubtful that treat would await us all.

GAME 1

BLUE JACKETS 4, CAPITALS 3

Here we go again? Caps blow lead

BY ISABELLE KHURSHUDYAN

Artemi Panarin did a victory lap around the Washington Capitals' zone, raising his arms as he skated in a circle and players in red jerseys dropped their heads and moved out of his way. He was this game's playoff hero, the latest image of Washington postseason disappointment.

The Capitals squandered a two-goal first-period lead and then another one-goal lead in the final five minutes of regulation before falling to the Columbus Blue Jackets in overtime, 4-3, in the first game of the Eastern Conference quarterfinal series. The blame is easy to place: three penalties in the third period that led to two power-play goals.

"You've got a lead there, you've got to be smart," Capitals goaltender Philipp Grubauer said. "Don't make it hard on yourself basically. We kind of shot ourselves in the foot a little bit."

The Capitals took a 3-2 lead 5:12 into the third period when forwards Devante Smith-Pelly and Jakub Vrana streaked into the offensive zone, Vrana speeding and spinning around Columbus players before stopping at the goal line to send a perfect pass across the crease to Smith-Pelly. He smacked the puck past goaltender Sergei Bobrovsky, and chants of "D-S-P" followed. Washington, it seemed, had found its new playoff hero.

But the Capitals' lack of discipline spoiled that story line. Washington was clinging to a 2-1 lead at the start of the third period when forward Tom Wilson hit center Alexander Wennberg in the corner. Wennberg crumpled to the ice, and Wilson went to the box for charging. Columbus's power play was the seventh worst in the league during the regular season, but with Thomas Vanek left alone in front of the crease, he beat Grubauer just 13 seconds into the man-advantage.

Wennberg, meanwhile, suffered an "upper-body" injury on Wilson's hit and did not return.

"I'm just trying to finish my check there," Wilson said. "I'm obviously not trying to take a penalty. That cost us the game. That's a critical moment. I've got to be better and maybe pass up on that hit. We've got the lead there, so maybe a big hit's not needed."

After Smith-Pelly lifted the Capitals to a lead, Washington was called for two more penalties. Forward Andre Burakovsky's tripping infraction with less than five minutes left in the game was the costly one, as Seth Jones tied the game to force overtime.

Grubauer, in just the second playoff start of his career, allowed three goals on 25 shots in regulation, and 12 of the shots he faced had been on the power play. He beat out Braden Holtby, a Vezina Trophy winner, for the top job, but the two had split time in net for the last month in the regular season. Coach Barry Trotz said Grubauer's play was "fine," and he didn't commit to sticking with him for Sunday's Game 2.

"Right now, I'm going to reevaluate that," Trotz said. "Philipp's body of work has been good. ... We'll sit down and reevaluate all the goals, evaluate our team and where we're at and go from there."

Before the Capitals unraveled with costly penalties, it had been a Blue Jackets infraction that had cost Columbus dearly in the first period. The Blue Jackets were one of the league's most disciplined teams during the regular season, called for the second-fewest minor penalties. But the game turned on a boarding major assessed to Columbus's Josh Anderson, who hit Capitals defenseman Michal Kempny into the glass with 2:37 left in the first period.

Kempny was down on the ice in apparent distress, eventually skating off with the team trainer, who held a towel to Kempny's face. He didn't return, and his status going forward is unclear, a potential blow to a blue line that had been stabilized by his arrival just before the late February trade deadline.

Anderson, who scored 19 goals with 11 assists this season, was ejected, and Washington got a five-minute power play.

The Capitals' man-advantage unit needed just 29 seconds to score, Evgeny Kuznetsov's shot getting tipped by Blue Jackets defenseman Ryan Murray to redirect the puck through Bobrovsky's legs.

Washington still had more than four minutes of power-play time remaining, and 29 seconds after his first goal, Kuznetsov scored a second, firing from the left faceoff circle on a rush into the zone. The Capitals went to first intermission with a 2-0 lead and 2:23 of power-play time to start the second period.

"There was plenty of game left," Blue Jackets Coach John Tortorella said. "We just knew we just had to stay with it. We're still took too many penalties."

But Washington bailed out Columbus with penalties of its own. The two teams had never met before in the playoffs, each battling its own postseason demons. The Blue Jackets are chasing a first series victory in franchise history. The Capitals have won plenty of first-round series, but they haven't gotten past the second round in two decades.

"You've got to be smarter," Wilson said. "That's playoff hockey, that's what it's all about is momentum and not giving the other team life in crucial moments of the game. There's some situations out there that we can obviously manage better."

APRIL 12 AT WASHINGTON

Columbus	**0**	**1**	**2**	**1**	**4**
Washington	**2**	**0**	**1**	**0**	**3**

FIRST PERIOD

Scoring: 1, Washington, Kuznetsov 1 (Backstrom, Carlson), 17:52 (pp). 2, Washington, Kuznetsov 2 (Backstrom, Carlson), 18:21 (pp).

SECOND PERIOD

Scoring: 3, Columbus, Wennberg 1 (Jenner, Vanek), 4:48.

THIRD PERIOD

Scoring: 4, Columbus, Vanek 1 (Panarin, Dubois), 1:31 (pp). 5, Washington, Smith-Pelly 1 (Carlson, Vrana), 5:12. 6, Columbus, Jones 1 (Panarin, Atkinson), 15:34 (pp).

OVERTIME

Scoring: 7, Columbus, Panarin 1 (Cole, Dubois), 6:02.

SHOTS ON GOAL

Columbus	4	12	9	2	27
Washington	9	16	5	0	30

Power-play opportunities: Columbus 2 of 4; Washington 2 of 6.

Goalies: Columbus, Bobrovsky 1-0 (30 shots-27 saves). Washington, Grubauer 0-1 (27-23).

Capitals goalie Philipp Grubauer was unable to stop Artemi Panarin's shot in overtime, and Coach Barry Trotz didn't commit to sticking with him. (PHOTOS BY JOHN MCDONNELL)

GAME 2

BLUE JACKETS 5, CAPITALS 4

Feeling blue after second loss at home

BY ISABELLE KHURSHUDYAN

Fans stood, waited and stared at the scoreboard to learn their team's fate. The Washington Capitals stayed seated on the bench as officials huddled around an iPad with headsets on. Like most everyone else, the players squinted up to see the replays, a sinking feeling settling in with each closer look at Matt Calvert's skate and if it was onside.

"You couldn't quite tell if his skate was up or not — we were sort of hoping and praying it was," Capitals Coach Barry Trotz said. "But I didn't feel good about it, that we were going to get a call there."

Calls had defined the game to that point, some forcing the Capitals to lose their grip on it before others got them back into it. The referee skated out to center ice and delivered Washington's unfortunate news. The overtime game-winning goal from Calvert was onside, and that meant the Capitals had lost, 5-4, in Game 2 of their first-round Stanley Cup playoff series against the Columbus Blue Jackets at Capital One Arena on Sunday night.

Now Washington is in an 0-2 series hole, having lost both games at home with the next two at Columbus's Nationwide Arena. For a second straight game, the Capitals squandered a two-goal lead. For the second straight game, Washington fell in overtime. For a fourth straight season, the team is now on the precipice of another postseason disappointment that ends short of the conference finals.

"It's hard," captain Alex Ovechkin said. "Obviously, we have opportunities to finish it up, but we didn't two games in a row."

The Capitals have played eight first-round playoff games the past two seasons, and seven of those have gone to overtime, hockey's ulcer-inducing version of a coin flip. For the second time in two games this series, Washington ended up on the wrong side of it. A veteran team will once again have to ask itself what could have been had it played more responsibly against a club that's never won a playoff series.

"We need to be a little smarter," center Nicklas Backstrom said. "We need to play with better discipline — especially when we have the lead twice. There is where we have to get better. And we have to play for 60 minutes. They're a good team, and obviously they've shown these last two games that they're never going to give up. So it's going to be a battle with them. Unfortunately we're down 2-0."

Capital One Arena was a cacophony of cowbells, chants, horns and groans Sunday night, but it's the whistles that the Capitals might remember most. Three days after the team blew a two-goal lead because it took too many penalties, it again blew a two-goal lead because of the same problem. But after Columbus went ahead late in the second period, the Blue Jackets did Washington a favor and were called for three minor penalties of their own in the third.

On the third power-play try of the period, the Capitals finally broke through to tie the game. T.J. Oshie beat goaltender Sergei Bobrovsky from the slot with 3:35 left in regulation. Bobrovsky had saved a whopping 20 shots in the period, but the one from Oshie marked Washington's third man-advantage tally of the game and its fifth of the series.

Apparently not learning their lesson in Thursday's 4-3 overtime loss to the Blue Jackets, the Capitals were again stung by their own lack of discipline. After Josh Anderson cut Washington's second-period lead to one goal on a five-on-two rush at goaltender Philipp Grubauer, Capitals forward Tom Wilson was called for roughing after a post-whistle skirmish in front of Washington's net. Wilson's actions were unnecessary, and while the home fans booed, the call stood nonetheless. In Game 1, the Blue Jackets had tied the game with Wilson in the box. They did the same Sunday night, with Cam Atkinson scoring his second goal of the game on the power play to make it 3-3.

Then, with 2:20 left in the second period, Devante Smith-Pelly went to the box for holding the stick, and Zach Werenski's point shot on the power play beat Grubauer to lift the Blue Jackets to a 4-3 lead before second intermission. Grubauer had allowed four goals on 22 shots, and as the team came out of the tunnel for the third period, it was goaltender Braden Holtby leading the way.

"I don't think I played that good," Grubauer said. "The last one was on me."

Neither Washington netminder could help the Capitals beat Bobrovsky, however, as he finished with 54 saves.

"At the end of the day, you look at the two sides, and Bob was the difference today for them," Trotz said. "He was on his game, and we just needed that one save. We just needed that one save, and we weren't able to get it."

In his first game back from an undisclosed "upper-body" injury, fourth-line center Jay Beagle gave the Capitals an unexpected offensive lift Sunday. He deflected defenseman Brooks Orpik's shot into the net just 2:12 into the game. That marked Beagle's seventh goal in 63 career playoff games. Washington then extended its lead with a familiar source of offense. After Atkinson was called for goaltender interference, the Capitals' power play took advantage with an Ovechkin one-timer from his sweet spot in the left faceoff circle.

Ovechkin had been disappointed with his play in Thursday's game, too quiet for the NHL's leading goal-scorer during the regular season. His first power-play goal Sunday gave Washington a 2-0 lead less than 14 minutes into the game. The Blue Jackets didn't take long to answer. Atkinson got behind defenseman Dmitry Orlov on a breakaway, patiently waiting out Grubauer to tuck the puck into the small opening between Grubauer's skate and the goal post. That made it 2-1 after the first period, but Ovechkin again came through with another vintage shot from the left circle on the power play.

With the Capitals up by two goals again, they imploded once again by taking penalties, a familiar refrain for springtime hockey in this city. Now the team has to hope the Blue Jackets' two-game lead is as dangerous as a two-goal one has been for Washington.

"Our group has a lot of fight in it, and we're not going away," Trotz said. "We're not going away. We're going to be around, and you're going to see us dig in. And you're going to see us fight. And you're going to see us make something happen here. I really believe in the group, and I'm excited to get to Columbus and I'm excited for Game 3."

APRIL 15 AT WASHINGTON

Columbus	**1**	**3**	**0**	**1**	**5**
Washington	**2**	**1**	**1**	**0**	**4**

FIRST PERIOD

Scoring: 1, Washington, Beagle 1 (Orpik, Jerabek), 2:12. 2, Washington, Ovechkin 1 (Oshie, Carlson), 13:26 (pp). 3, Columbus, Atkinson 1 (Foligno), 18:25.

SECOND PERIOD

Scoring: 4, Washington, Ovechkin 2 (Backstrom, Carlson), 4:09 (pp). 5, Columbus, Anderson 1 (Jones, Werenski), 8:49. 6, Columbus, Atkinson 2 (Panarin, Jones), 11:13 (pp). 7, Columbus, Werenski 1 (Panarin, Bjorkstrand), 18:52 (pp).

THIRD PERIOD

Scoring: 8, Washington, Oshie 1 (Carlson, Backstrom), 16:25 (pp).

OVERTIME

Scoring: 9, Columbus, Calvert 1 (Werenski, Anderson), 12:22.

SHOTS ON GOAL

Columbus	8	14	5	3	30
Washington	19	12	21	6	58

Power-play opportunities: Columbus 2 of 4; Washington 3 of 7.

Goalies: Columbus, Bobrovsky 2-0 (58 shots-54 saves). Washington, Grubauer 0-1 (22-18), Holtby 0-1 (8-7).

Nicklas Backstrom, taking the ice for Game 2, had two assists in the losing effort. (PHOTO BY TONI L. SANDYS)

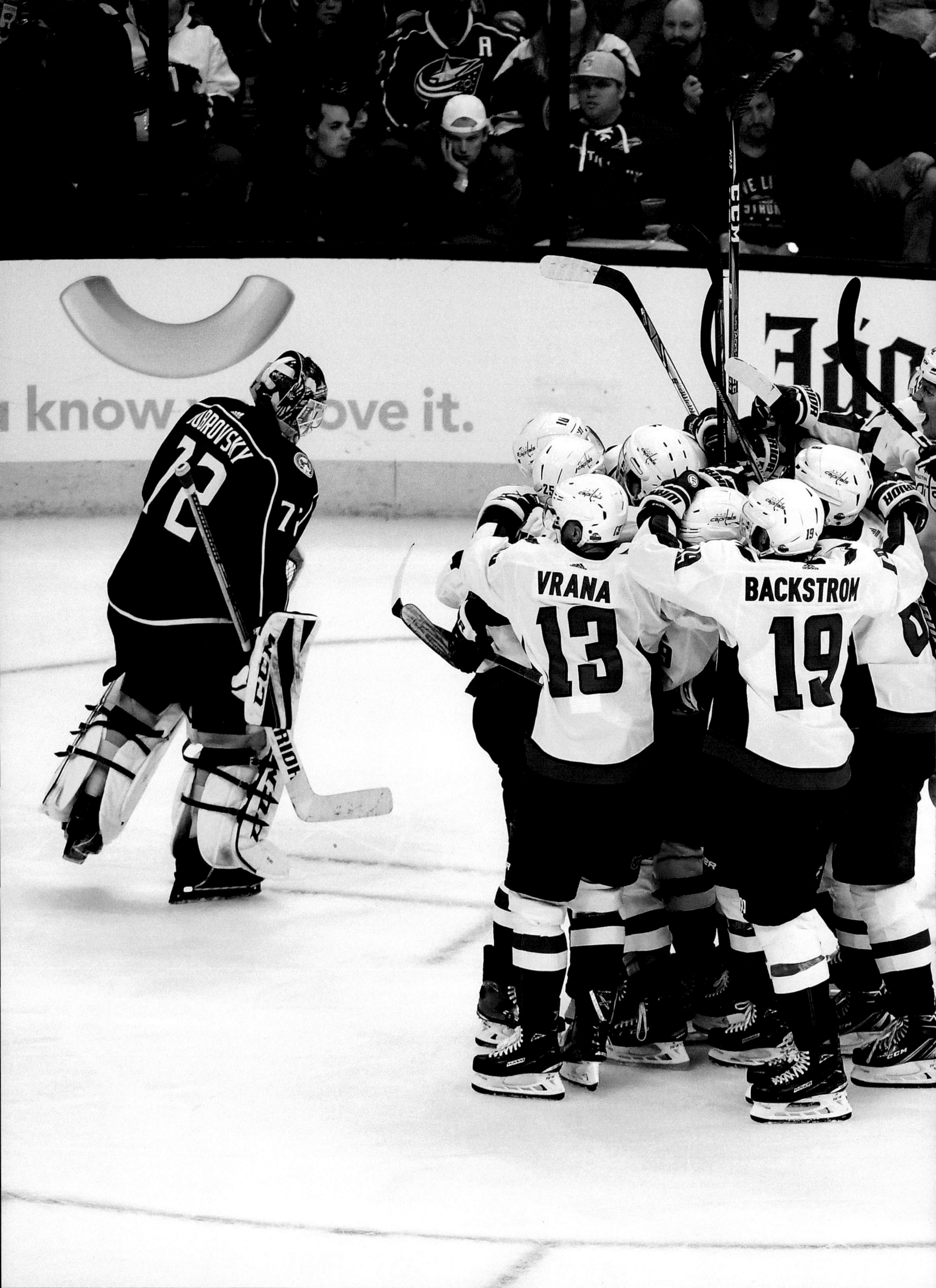

BOBROVSKY
72
VRANA
13
BACKSTROM
19
CCM

GAME 3

CAPITALS 3, BLUE JACKETS 2

Ugly goal gives Caps first win of playoffs

BY ISABELLE KHURSHUDYAN

A puck finally bounced Washington's way when Lars Eller scored in the second overtime, giving the visitors a reason to celebrate. (PHOTO BY JONATHAN NEWTON)

APRIL 17 AT COLUMBUS

Washington	0	2	0	0	1	3
Columbus	0	1	1	0	0	2

FIRST PERIOD
Scoring: None.

SECOND PERIOD
Scoring: 1, Washington, Wilson 1 (Niskanen, Ovechkin), 5:52. 2, Columbus, Dubois 1 (Panarin, Jones), 11:18. 3, Washington, Carlson 1 (Ovechkin, Backstrom), 14:43 (pp).

THIRD PERIOD
Scoring: 4, Columbus, Panarin 2 (Atkinson), 4:12.

OVERTIME
Scoring: None.

2ND OVERTIME
Scoring: 5, Washington, Eller 1 (Connolly, Smith-Pelly), 9:00.

SHOTS ON GOAL

Washington	11	14	6	6	8	45
Columbus	9	7	10	7	2	35

Power-play opportunities:
Washington 1 of 4; Columbus 0 of 4.

Goalies: Washington, Holtby 1-1 (35 shots-33 saves). Columbus, Bobrovsky 2-1 (45-42).

Braden Holtby walked out to the Washington Capitals' bench an hour before puck drop Tuesday night carrying his stick with him. He leaned his forearm and chin on the blade, staring at an empty sheet of ice in an empty arena. It's a pregame ritual when he starts, a peaceful few minutes before he is the last line of defense for what can often be chaos in front of him.

When Holtby took his place in the patch of blue paint, Columbus Blue Jackets fans mockingly sang his name. Pucks bounced off and around him. As Game 3 of this first-round Stanley Cup playoff series became a marathon, two-overtime whirlwind, Holtby was the picture of poise, steady as everything else was shaking.

Then, exactly nine minutes into the second extra period, Lars Eller scored on a rebound, and the Capitals' playoff hopes went from dismal to slightly less so. Washington won, 3-2, and cut Columbus's series lead to two games to one. Holtby finally left his net after a brilliant 33-save performance, joining the Capitals' wild celebration on the other end of the ice.

Holtby's journey to that moment had been about as wild as Tuesday night's game. He went from being Washington's no-doubt No. 1 goaltender, a Vezina Trophy winner just two years ago, to struggling so much in the second half of the season that he was on the bench to start the playoffs. As the Capitals found their groove again with their first win of the postseason, so too did their goaltender. He weathered four Blue Jackets power plays, including one in the first overtime.

"It's pretty normal in my eyes," defenseman John Carlson said. "I think he did a great job playing the puck, stopping the puck. Yeah, he probably hasn't had his best stuff like we're normally seeing, Vezina-type seasons. But you win the Vezina, you're capable of being a pretty good goalie, and there was no drop in confidence from us. He's a battler, and that's what he did."

A sold-out Nationwide Arena had been quiet to start the third period as the Capitals led by a goal. Then Dmitry Orlov committed an offensive-zone turnover, and Blue Jackets forwards Artemi Panarin and Cam Atkinson raced up the ice with just Carlson back. Panarin passed to Atkinson. Atkinson passed to Panarin.

Panarin shot into a half-open net as Holtby split from one side of the crease to the other trying to follow the rapid puck movement.

White towels waved. The arena's infamous goal cannon went off. Then the "Holtby" chants started. For the third game in a row, the Capitals and Blue Jackets were tied late. Eight of the Capitals' past nine games in a first-round series have gone to overtime.

"We're mature in that area, if you will," Coach Barry Trotz said. "They're exciting games. There's two good teams here. There's very little separation."

Considering this was effectively a must-win game for the Capitals because just four teams have ever recovered from a three-games-to-none deficit, Columbus looked just as desperate as Washington, if not more so. In front of their home fans, the Blue Jackets tasted the opportunity to inch closer to the organization's first series win. The Capitals caught a break when Panarin's slap shot in the final two minutes of regulation went off a goal post, sending the teams to a third straight overtime. When that didn't decide it, a second overtime period came.

"I think the first overtime, you're a little more focused," forward Tom Wilson said. "Second overtime, a few more jokes come out, and it's a little lighter."

With both teams fatigued after having played essentially an extra game with four overtimes in three games, Eller's goal was exactly the kind of fluky tally that happens after 89 minutes of hockey. Brett Connolly put a shot on net, and Eller went for the rebound. The puck bounced off Columbus defenseman Zach Werenski's leg, then off Eller's skate and then past goaltender Sergei Bobrovsky.

"It was a real ugly OT-winner goal," Eller said. "I had a feeling it was going be one of those. It doesn't make the win less sweet."

After allowing four goals on 22 shots through two periods in Game 2 on Sunday

Alex Ovechkin, warming up for Game 3, had two assists as the Caps got back in the series. (PHOTO BY JONATHAN NEWTON)

night, goaltender Philipp Grubauer was benched for Holtby, who has the second-best all-time career postseason save percentage. Holtby had struggled in the second half of this season, and he was eventually unseated as the team's starting goaltender because Grubauer outplayed him down the stretch. But Holtby had improved over the final month, and Trotz put him back in net for Tuesday's game, his 60th postseason start.

"There was still some rust at times," said Holtby, who had previously started a game 10 days ago.

Holtby had especially struggled through February; he was 2-5-2 with an .873 save percentage and 4.62 goals against average. He allowed three goals on nine shots in a game at Anaheim and was yanked in the second period, the third time he had been pulled in a stretch of six starts. The next day in Los Angeles, Trotz told Holtby he would be starting Grubauer for the next week because he wanted Holtby to have a "reset" period to work on his game. Trotz said Holtby had gotten "away from some of the foundations" that made him one of the best goaltenders in the league for four years.

With Washington on the edge of disaster after losing the first two games of the series at home, Trotz trusted Holtby to backstop a Capitals comeback.

"He had a chance to come in down in the series, and he's a competitor, one of our leaders," Wilson said. "I think the season got away from him a little. It wasn't like he was playing badly, you know? He drops a couple games, Grubi comes in and is playing phenomenal and then you have that kind of controversy. That's hard on a goalie. They're good friends, but it's hard when you have a guy right behind you who's playing unbelievable. You maybe fight the pucks a little more.

"But I think that looked like the Holts that we all know. It's great to see."

27
19
19
capitals
WARRIOR

GAME 4

CAPITALS 4, BLUE JACKETS 1

All tied up: Ovechkin's prediction comes true

BY ISABELLE KHURSHUDYAN

T.J. Oshie hoisted Alex Ovechkin after scoring in the second period of Game 4 at Columbus. (PHOTO BY JONATHAN NEWTON)

APRIL 19 AT COLUMBUS

Washington	**1**	**1**	**2**	**4**
Columbus	**0**	**0**	**1**	**1**

FIRST PERIOD

Scoring: 1, Washington, Wilson 2 (Kuznetsov), 6:16.

SECOND PERIOD

Scoring: 2, Washington, Oshie 2 (Ovechkin, Carlson), 9:19 (pp).

THIRD PERIOD

Scoring: 3, Washington, Ovechkin 3 (Wilson, Kuznetsov), 2:49. 4, Columbus, Jenner 1 (Anderson), 6:22. 5, Washington, Kuznetsov 3, 17:41.

SHOTS ON GOAL

Washington	12	13	8	33
Columbus	7	8	9	24

Power-play opportunities: Washington 1 of 3; Columbus 0 of 3.

Goalies: Washington, Holtby 2-1 (24 shots-23 saves). Columbus, Bobrovsky 2-2 (32-29).

Alex Ovechkin now can add prophet to his impressive résumé.

When the Capitals found themselves in a hole after losing the first two games of their first-round Stanley Cup playoff series at home, Ovechkin matter-of-factly said the team would return to Washington for a Game 5 with the series tied. He repeated himself Tuesday morning before the team won Game 3 against the Columbus Blue Jackets in double overtime.

Then, in the third period Thursday night, he ensured he would be right, scoring the Capitals' third goal in a 4-1 win over the Blue Jackets, the first game of the series to be decided in regulation. The Capitals have stormed back, winning both games at Nationwide Arena to set up a return to Capital One Arena on Saturday tied at two games apiece and with home-ice advantage restored.

Though Ovechkin was most vocal in his confidence, the rest of the locker room shared his belief.

"There was no other option," goaltender Braden Holtby said. "Our goal is to win a Stanley Cup, and that's what we viewed as our best chance after losing the first two. We've been a confident group all year — I think that's been our strongest asset — so I don't think we've ever doubted ourselves."

Washington has Holtby most to thank for the comeback. After he was initially beaten out by Philipp Grubauer to start the series, Holtby has shined in his return to the cage. He made 33 saves in Tuesday's win, and though he saw fewer shots Thursday night, he was arguably sharper, so positionally sound that he barely seemed to be moving as he stopped several point-blank Columbus shots. The one goal he allowed, scored by Blue Jackets winger Boone Jenner, came when Washington already was up 3-0. He finished with 23 saves.

Though Columbus Coach John Tortorella thought his team played better than the Capitals in Game 3 despite the result, his assessment of the Blue Jackets after Thursday's game was succinct. "We laid an egg," he said repeatedly.

"It's safe to say that was our most complete game from top to bottom," Capitals forward T.J. Oshie said. "That's something that we want to build on, and you can see at the end, when they scored that [Jenner] goal, it was like nothing even happened and we just kept going. That's the kind of feeling you get when you're playing consistent, deep hockey."

Ovechkin has a history of postseason guarantees. Just three years ago, he said the Capitals would beat the New York Rangers in Game 7 to advance to the Eastern Conference final. That didn't pan out, but Ovechkin has been confident in this team since training camp, even when external expectations were down. "We're not going to be suck," he said in September, and despite significant offseason roster turnover that had Washington leaning on more rookies in the lineup, the team won its division for a third straight year, largely because Ovechkin scored a league-high 49 goals.

Pessimism for Washington's season returned when the Capitals lost their first two playoff games at home. But Ovechkin was so sure the team would respond that he said it twice.

"That just shows confidence that we're confident we can do it," Coach Barry Trotz said Wednesday. "But you can say it as much as you want. Now you've got to back it up."

While Washington's power play has been strong this series with six goals in the first three games, the Capitals' stars had yet to impress at even strength. The Blue Jackets entered Thursday's game with four five-on-five goals from their top line anchored by 19-year-old center Pierre-Luc Dubois, and the Capitals had just one goal from their first line — Tom Wilson's tip in the last game. Meanwhile, Washington's second line with center Nicklas Backstrom and Oshie had yet to score at even strength.

Wilson came through for a second straight game. Defenseman John Carlson and

Chandler Stephenson had a two-on-one, and after Sergei Bobrovsky saved Carlson's shot, Stephenson's attempt to put in the rebound was foiled by Columbus forward Thomas Vanek, who was sprawled across the goal line. Vanek gloved the puck away, but Capitals center Evgeny Kuznetsov corralled it, setting up a Wilson one-timer to lift the Capitals to a 1-0 lead 6:16 into the game.

Washington has scored first in every game this series, but it has struggled to maintain the lead. The Capitals got their third power play of the game 8:49 into the second period, when Blue Jackets sniper Artemi Panarin was whistled for slashing Kuznetsov. Washington's man-advantage has scored in every game this series, and it came through again. Ovechkin took two shots, but it was Oshie's whack at the rebound that got past Bobrovsky to make it a 2-0 Washington lead.

"You're up two or three goals in the playoffs, it can be tedious," Wilson said. "The other team is coming. They're taking chances. We did a good job at making the plays that we needed to and getting odd-man rushes."

A two-goal cushion has spelled trouble for the Capitals this series, and it's often referred to as the most dangerous lead in hockey. They squandered that very lead in the first two games, falling in overtime both times. But then Ovechkin scored 2:49 into the third period, pushing the Capitals' lead to three goals for the first time in the four games.

That was insurance for what Ovechkin believed would happen all along: The Capitals are returning home with the series tied.

Alex Ovechkin predicted the Caps would win the series, and his goal in Game 4 helped make it happen. (PHOTO BY JONATHAN NEWTON)

Coors LIGHT
DUNKIN'
WARRIOR
WARRIOR
19

GAME 5

CAPITALS 4, BLUE JACKETS 3

For first time, Caps are right at home

BY ISABELLE KHURSHUDYAN

Nicklas Backstrom scored two goals in Game 5, including the winner 11:53 into overtime. (PHOTO BY TONI L. SANDYS)

APRIL 21 AT WASHINGTON

Columbus	**1**	**1**	**1**	**0**	**3**
Washington	**1**	**2**	**0**	**1**	**4**

FIRST PERIOD

Scoring: 1, Columbus, Calvert 2 (Jones), 10:08 (sh). 2, Washington, Backstrom 1 (Kempny, Stephenson), 13:22.

SECOND PERIOD

Scoring: 3, Washington, Kuznetsov 4 (Orlov), 3:21. 4, Columbus, Calvert 3, 4:45. 5, Washington, Oshie 3 (Carlson, Backstrom), 16:42 (pp).

THIRD PERIOD

Scoring: 6, Columbus, Bjorkstrand 1 (Wennberg, Cole), 2:30.

OVERTIME

Scoring: 7, Washington, Backstrom 2 (Orlov, Stephenson), 11:53.

SHOTS ON GOAL

Columbus	11	9	16	6	42
Washington	7	13	1	8	29

Power-play opportunities: Columbus 0 of 5; Washington 1 of 4.

Goalies: Columbus, Bobrovsky 2-3 (29 shots-25 saves). Washington, Holtby 2-1 (42-39).

Capital One Arena had been a springtime house of horrors for the Washington Capitals lately. An impressive regular season had assured the team home-ice advantage through the first two rounds of the Stanley Cup playoffs, but after just the first two games of their first-round series against the Columbus Blue Jackets, it seemed the Capitals would be better off playing away from the District. With anxious red-clad fans in the stands, the Capitals had lost Games 1 and 2 at home to fall into a disastrous hole.

They had seemed more at ease on the road, storming back to tie the series before a pivotal Game 5 back in Washington on Saturday afternoon. Those red-clad fans groaned when the puck bounced around in Washington's end too long. They cheered when Braden Holtby made one spectacular save after another. They threw their hands up in frustration when Sergei Bobrovsky did the same on the other end of the ice.

And then they jumped for joy when Nicklas Backstrom's stick smacked Dmitry Orlov's shot at just the right time, deflecting the puck to plop into the Columbus net 11:53 into overtime. The Capitals were jumping with them, the bench clearing as the team celebrated in a corner. With Washington's 4-3 overtime win, the Capitals now have a three-games-to-two series lead over the Blue Jackets and are one win away from advancing to the second round.

"We've been playing some good hockey," said Backstrom, who scored his first two goals of the postseason Saturday. "Hopefully we can bring our confidence to Columbus on Monday."

Washington entered the third period with a 3-2 edge, but the team has struggled to protect leads for most of the series. On an extended shift in the Capitals' zone, center Evgeny Kuznetsov attempted to clear the puck out but Columbus's Alexander Wennberg was able to keep it in. A point shot by Blue Jackets defenseman Ian Cole was redirected by Oliver Bjorkstrand, tying the game once again 2:30 into the period. Though Washington wasn't losing, the energy seemed to drain out of the arena. The hosts didn't record their first shot on goal in the period until 11:39 into it.

That shot was the only one the Capitals managed in the third period, while the Blue Jackets fired off 16. Washington had flatlined to end regulation, fortunate to have an intermission to regroup as it prepared to play overtime for the fourth time in five games.

"We just said, 'Hey, let's get on our toes and let's go for it,'" Coach Barry Trotz said. "That's what we've wanted to do when we've got into the playoffs: Go for it. We've done that in overtimes. As I was leaving the [locker] room after the period, I could hear the right guys all saying the right things."

Said defenseman John Carlson: "We came out as a new team in overtime."

Bobrovsky might have been bored in the third period, but he certainly looked sharp early in overtime. He stopped an Alex Ovechkin one-timer from the high slot and then gloved a Carlson wrist shot from point-blank range. Holtby answered with his own fantastic sequence of saves, and a duel in net played out through nearly 12 minutes of the extra period. Holtby was ultimately better, winning his third straight playoff start after making 39 saves.

"I've played enough against him to know he's going to come up with big saves every game," Holtby said. "That's who he is. As a fellow goaltender, I just try and

block out as much as I can. What happens at the other end of the ice has absolutely nothing to do with my job. I'm just focusing on my job because I know he's going to do his. That's just part of knowing your role, knowing how to prepare to play your best."

Entering Saturday afternoon, the Capitals had lost five of their past six home playoff games dating back to last season's second round against the Pittsburgh Penguins. Players had admitted feeling some extra pressure playing in front of their home fans. Through regulation, Game 5 had been the worst game Washington had played in the series.

But overtime was a chance for the Capitals to regroup in their home locker room. The team in the visiting dressing room left Capital One Arena disappointed but confident this wouldn't be its last game in this building.

"We'll be back here for Game 7," Columbus Coach John Tortorella said.

"What else are you going to say?" Trotz said. "That's good. He wants to get it out there that he believes in his team, just as I believe in my team. It's our job not to let that happen."

Blue Jackets goalie Sergei Bobrovsky looked back helplessly after the Capitals' Nicklas Backstrom scored the winning goal in overtime. (PHOTO BY TONI L. SANDYS)

WASHINGTON
capitals
43
CCM

GAME 6

CAPITALS 6, BLUE JACKETS 3

Backs to the wall, Caps bust through

BY ISABELLE KHURSHUDYAN

Alex Ovechkin scored twice in the second period to help Washington win its fourth in a row and finish off Columbus. (PHOTO BY TONI L. SANDYS)

APRIL 23 AT COLUMBUS

	1	2	3	
Capitals	**1**	**2**	**3**	**6**
Blue Jackets	**0**	**1**	**2**	**3**

FIRST PERIOD

Scoring: 1, Washington, Orlov 1 (Stephenson, Niskanen), 12:12.

SECOND PERIOD

Scoring: 2, Columbus, Foligno 1 (Murray, Cole), 8:40. 3, Washington, Ovechkin 4 (Orpik, Djoos), 12:50. 4, Washington, Ovechkin 5 (Carlson, Kuznetsov), 18:23 (pp).

THIRD PERIOD

Scoring: 5, Columbus, Dubois 2 (Calvert), 2:25. 6, Washington, Smith-Pelly 2, 3:56. 7, Washington, Stephenson 1 (Beagle, Orpik), 5:30 (sh). 8, Columbus, Foligno 2 (Jenner, Bjorkstrand), 8:22. 9, Washington, Eller 2 (Beagle), 19:46 (en).

SHOTS ON GOAL

Capitals	10	12	6	28
Blue Jackets	7	14	17	38

Power-play opportunities:
Washington 1 of 3;
Columbus 0 of 4.

Goalies:
Washington, Holtby 3-1 (38 shots-35 saves). Columbus, Bobrovsky 2-3 (27-22).

The Washington Capitals celebrated like it was any other victory. Goaltender Braden Holtby straightened in net as his teammates calmly left the bench and skated over to hug him one by one. The mood in the locker room was happy but subdued.

Washington beat the Columbus Blue Jackets, 6-3, in Game 6 to win the first-round Stanley Cup playoff series between the teams, four games to two. For a team that seemed to accomplish so much, the Capitals merely met their own high expectations.

"I think we accomplished what we believed we could from the start of the series," Holtby said nonchalantly. "Obviously, enjoy it for a bit, rest up and prepare for the next one."

After falling into an early 2-0 series hole, losing both of the first two games at home, the Capitals won four straight playoff games, three of which were on the road, for the first time since 1990 to advance to the second round for the fourth consecutive season, a first in franchise history.

The journey to this point was rockier with a roster that is less talented and less experienced, but after experiencing growing pains throughout the season, Washington is back to exactly where it was last season, preparing for a second-round series against the defending Stanley Cup champion Pittsburgh Penguins. As they were in this series and throughout this season, the Capitals are confident in the face of external doubt.

"Obviously, you never know what's going to happen, but we just believed in each other," said captain Alex Ovechkin, who scored two goals. "There was no panic. We knew that we'd have to take one game at a time. ... We started believing more. We could see everybody stepping up and playing great hockey and give us success."

In the six games against Columbus, Washington rode its stars on a power play that scored in every game, a goaltender who had initially been beaten out for the starting job and secondary scoring that came through in the timeliest of moments. Game 6 was a culmination of all three, as the Capitals answered every Blue Jackets push with one of their own.

Washington had struggled to protect leads in this series, and Blue Jackets center Pierre-Luc Dubois's slap shot cut Washington's two-goal lead to one within the first three minutes of the third period. The Capitals responded quickly, once again deflating the crowd at Nationwide Arena. Third-line winger Devante Smith-Pelly scored his second goal of the series with a clear shot from the left faceoff circle on a rush to make it 4-2. Defenseman Christian Djoos was called for interference 4:39 into the period, but within a minute, Chandler Stephenson scored on a shorthanded breakaway to give the Capitals a three-goal cushion.

Washington then had to withstand a furious Columbus push for the final 14:30, what Holtby called the hardest period of hockey he had played. Blue Jackets captain Nick Foligno scored his second goal of the game with 11:38 to play, and an interference penalty by Evgeny Kuznetsov gave Columbus a late power play. The Capitals killed their 17th straight penalty in the series. Blue Jackets goaltender Sergei Bobrovsky was pulled for an extra attacker with three minutes left, and Washington survived that, too, capping the win with an empty-net goal by Lars Eller. Holtby finished with 35 saves.

"We've had lots of different adversity through this year than maybe in the past," Capitals Coach Barry Trotz said. "We've grown up a little bit in some ways that we understand our core group is really, really strong. They believe in each other."

After Washington had fallen into its 2-0 series deficit, Ovechkin matter-of-factly said the team would return to Capital One Arena with the series tied. The Capitals then won Games 3 and 4 in Columbus to back up Ovechkin's word. Trotz acknowledged that Columbus was the better team in Washington's Game 5 overtime win, and Blue Jackets Coach John Tortorella was so confident in his group that he twice said Columbus would return to Capital One Arena for Game 7.

After the Capitals closed out the series in Game 6, Tortorella repeatedly

Chandler Stephenson, center, had a shorthanded goal and an assist as the Caps rolled in Game 6. (PHOTO BY TONI L. SANDYS)

commented on how fiercely Washington had defended in the series. For most of the season, that appeared to be the team's greatest weakness because offseason roster turnover forced the Capitals to part with three blue-liners. The pairing of Dmitry Orlov and Matt Niskanen suffocated Columbus's top players, especially Artemi Panarin, who had seven points in the first three games and none after that. Djoos was a healthy scratch in the first two games and shined in the final four, assisting on Ovechkin's first goal of the game for his first point. Washington blocked 23 shots Monday.

"The better team won," Tortorella said. "Give them credit. I thought they played a complete game. We thought we might be able to get to them offensively, but they were stingy."

The defensive turning point in the series seemed to come with a change in net. The Capitals started goaltender Philipp Grubauer in the first two games, and after he had allowed eight goals in the two losses, Trotz turned to Holtby, the Vezina Trophy winner just two years ago. Though his struggles in the second half of the regular season caused him to lose the starting job to Grubauer, Holtby has the second-best all-time career save percentage in the playoffs. He entered Monday's game with an impressive .936 save percentage and 1.66 goals against average in this series, and he was Washington's best player as the team reeled off three straight wins to move to the verge of advancing.

Until the final second ticked off the clock Monday, Holtby was in position, his eyes on the puck. As Eller's empty-net goal sent fans to the exits in disappointment, Holtby took a knee with his mask lifted up, perhaps appreciating what he and his team had just pulled off. And then he pushed his mask back down and continued to go about his business.

"I think we've had a quiet confidence to ourselves that we just take it game by game this year," Holtby said. "That's what we did in the series. We didn't get too high or low. We just focused on the next game and believed we could win."

WASHINGTON
Capitals
CCM

2017-18 REGULAR SEASON

DIVISION CHAMPIONS

A big bet pays off

BY BARRY SVRLUGA

The Capitals finished atop the Metropolitan Division for the third straight year.
(PHOTO BY JONATHAN NEWTON)

The hangover is obvious. You can still smell the whiskey on the Washington Capitals' breath, feel the throbbing in their heads. The new season is here. The Caps can't shake the last. They're lamenting the opportunity past, the guys who are gone. The Pittsburgh Penguins and Game 7, and the pucks that didn't go in during that first period and the air sucked out of the building and ... it's all still here in October. Shouldn't be. But it is.

And yet they still have a team that opens the 13th season of Alex Ovechkin's career Thursday night in Ottawa, and that team has a future. Not just over the next six months and not just with Ovechkin.

For all the kvetching about the departures of Marcus Johansson and Karl Alzner and Justin Williams and Nate Schmidt, the Capitals' most significant moves of the summer revolved not around whom they let go but around whom they kept.

Ovechkin's contract runs through 2020-21. But T.J. Oshie and Evgeny Kuznetsov? They're now on the Caps' books — and, presumably, their roster — through 2024-25.

"Obviously," General Manager Brian MacLellan said this week, "we bet on a couple guys here."

With the bet comes a burden, one that can be spread around. Start with MacLellan, the man who built back-to-back Presidents' Trophy winners the past two years and now brings a lesser version of that roster into this season. The bet was on Oshie's intangibles and Kuznetsov's skill. And it was MacLellan's to own: eight years and $46 million for Oshie, eight years and $62.4 million for Kuznetsov.

The stakes are simple, and MacLellan knows it. In explaining the deal for Kuznetsov, he said: "If he's good, I'm good. If he's not, it was nice meeting you guys."

Only an executive's career on the line, then.

The contracts, though, have an impact on the players, too. They are no longer identified by the numbers 77 and 92, the digits on their jerseys. No, they now are linked inextricably to their salaries: Oshie and $46 million, Kuznetsov and $62 million. And they will be judged by those numbers above all else.

"There's a responsibility," Oshie said.

"It's about how a player is going to handle it, right?" Kuznetsov said.

As the Caps barreled through last season, with a Stanley Cup the only goal that mattered, Oshie, an unrestricted free agent at season's end, and Kuznetsov, who would be restricted, knew what awaited them. The goal of the Cup is unifying and dominating, but there's a lot of idle time on the road to sit and think, too.

"It never got in the way of my decision-making on the ice or my preparation," Oshie said. "But it creeps in. I thought about it. You have to. It's your future. I have a family."

As does Kuznetsov. Now those families are taken care of — and then some. How does a player respond to such security?

"I think it's tough because the player plays for the contract, and then he has a big year, and then there's a natural letdown," MacLellan said. "And then it becomes the pressure of the contract."

This phenomenon isn't unique to hockey. (Paging Albert Haynesworth.) Jayson Werth will finish his seven-year deal with the Nationals at some point in the coming weeks — he hopes, very late this month or very early next month — and is being warmly embraced by the fan base as he reminisces about helping turn a loser into a winner. But his first season in Washington was a dud, one in which he hit .232. He knew the fans were thinking, "We paid $126 million for this?" It bothered him, so he pressed. It was counterproductive.

Oshie and Kuznetsov need look only across their own locker room to find an example of how to handle their newfound riches, lifelong security — and the weight that comes with them. Nicklas Backstrom is entering the eighth year of a 10-year, $67 million deal. Find someone who thinks Backstrom has taken a shift or a practice off because of his contract, and I would like to meet him.

"Somehow you got to try to put that aside and be the guy you normally are," Backstrom said. "You know you can be a good player, and that's why they signed you for that number."

Simple enough. But also, this: "It's a lot mentally, too."

So MacLellan's bet is that Kuznetsov's talent, which has produced 97 assists the past two seasons combined, will continue to develop to the point that he is a perennial all-star candidate. His bet is that the production from Oshie's career year — 33 goals playing alongside Backstrom and Ovechkin — won't drop off significantly and more importantly that his leadership, experience, work ethic and competitive spirit will infiltrate the locker room even if he never scores 30 times again.

He is betting on the human beings wearing the skates.

"You try and do your homework," MacLellan said.

His homework showed that Mr. $46 Million and Mr. $62 Million — uh, Oshie and Kuznetsov — could handle all that comes with all those zeros. Each now knows what's ahead not just for himself but also for his family. Oshie's children are 3 and 1, and he and his wife love the fact that there are so many little ones "on the team," as Oshie said. There's a comfort level knowing his daughter is in the same preschool as Backstrom's little girl. Kuznetsov has one daughter and said he and his wife probably will have more children, so he can plan his life accordingly.

The contracts bring comfort, security and pressure, maybe in equal parts.

"Before I signed that deal, I knew it was going to be some pressure on me," Kuznetsov said. "But sometimes players need it. I think it's going to be even better for me."

Shake off last season, Caps fans. Shoot, shake off last season, Caps players and coaches and execs. There's a present here that matters. More than that, there's a future — a future that's tied to two players on whom the organization has placed a $108 million wager. Odds are, given the people to whom those numbers are attached, they will be fine.

2017-18 NHL STANDINGS

EASTERN CONFERENCE

METROPOLITAN	GP	W	L	OT	P
1. Washington	**82**	**49**	**26**	**7**	**105**
2. Pittsburgh	82	47	29	6	100
3. Philadelphia	82	42	26	14	98
4. Columbus	82	45	30	7	97
5. New Jersey	82	44	29	9	97
6. Carolina	82	36	35	11	83
7. N.Y. Islanders	82	35	37	10	80
8. N.Y. Rangers	82	34	39	9	77

ATLANTIC	GP	W	L	OT	P
1. Tampa Bay	82	54	23	5	113
2. Boston	82	50	20	12	112
3. Toronto	82	49	26	7	105
4. Florida	82	44	30	8	96
5. Detroit	82	30	39	13	73
6. Montreal	82	29	40	13	71
7. Ottawa	82	28	43	11	67
8. Buffalo	82	25	45	12	62

FIRST ROUND

Pittsburgh over Philadelphia, 4-2

Boston over Toronto, 4-3

Washington over Columbus, 4-2

Tampa Bay over New Jersey, 4-1

SECOND ROUND

Tampa Bay over Boston, 4-1

Washington over Pittsburgh, 4-2

CONFERENCE FINALS

Washington over Tampa Bay, 4-3

WESTERN CONFERENCE

PACIFIC	GP	W	L	OT	P
1. Vegas	82	51	24	7	109
2. Anaheim	82	44	25	13	101
3. San Jose	82	45	27	10	100
4. Los Angeles	82	45	29	8	98
5. Calgary	82	37	35	10	84
6. Edmonton	82	36	40	6	78
7. Vancouver	82	31	40	11	73
8. Arizona	82	29	41	12	70

CENTRAL	GP	W	L	OT	P
1. Nashville	82	53	18	11	117
2. Winnipeg	82	52	20	10	114
3. Minnesota	82	45	26	11	101
4. Colorado	82	43	30	9	95
5. St. Louis	82	44	32	6	94
6. Dallas	82	42	32	8	92
7. Chicago	82	33	39	10	76

FIRST ROUND

San Jose over Anaheim, 4-0

Winnipeg over Minnesota, 4-1

Vegas over Los Angeles, 4-0

Nashville over Colorado, 4-2

SECOND ROUND

Winnipeg over Nashville, 4-3

Vegas over San Jose, 4-2

CONFERENCE FINALS

Vegas over Winnipeg, 4-1

(ILLUSTRATIONS BY CRISTIANO SIQUEIRA)

Braden
Holtby

THE GOALTENDER

BRADEN HOLTBY

He leads with his head, and Caps follow

BY ISABELLE KHURSHUDYAN

A popular vacation destination, Kelowna, B.C., is on the eastern shore of Okanagan Lake with a waterfront downtown that's surrounded by parks, mountains and vineyards. It was where Washington Capitals goaltender Braden Holtby and new goaltending coach Scott Murray took a summer bonding trip of sorts, three days to get to know each other better in one of the most idyllic cities in Canada.

"It was good to get a plan in place for what we wanted to accomplish this year, and then also get something to work on ... and kind of have one aspect that we're going to work on through the year," Holtby said.

That one aspect would be the focus of Murray's goaltending teaching, a style called "head trajectory" that was developed by British Columbia-based Lyle Mast, who consults with several goalies and coaches in the NHL. The simplest way to describe head trajectory is tracking a puck with the head rather than just with the eyes. While in Kelowna, Holtby and Murray met with Mast to learn more about head trajectory and, as Holtby put it, "to see if there was any tools we could add."

Murray is the fifth goaltending coach Holtby has had in his seven-year tenure with the Capitals, and each has his own philosophies about the position. The transition from Mitch Korn to Murray was relatively seamless; Murray had started working with Washington's goalies last season when he was still the assistant goaltending coach and primarily responsible for the organization's minor league netminders.

But through those changes, Holtby has had to balance keeping an open mind to new ideas and concepts while sticking to a foundation that has made him a Vezina Trophy winner as one of the league's best and most consistent goaltenders the past three years.

"You pick and choose what works for you," Holtby said. "Obviously, everyone at this level has something that makes them successful that they bring to the table. A goaltending coach is like a teacher, and if you're going to broaden your horizons and broaden your game as much as you can, you want to get different teachers. You want to go to different classes and that kind of thing, learn everything about the position. And then you take all of that information and find what works for you. If you have one ideology in mind, you're not going to adapt to the changes in the game. Teams figure you out and your tendencies, so you've got to keep evolving."

Holtby and Korn took a similar trip together the summer before they first started their partnership in the 2014-15 season. That excursion featured some vision training with an optometrist in Minneapolis, and it was Korn, now the Capitals' director of goaltending, who suggested Holtby and Murray go to Kelowna together to start building their relationship and also explore the head-trajectory concept with Mast.

"Obviously, when you enter a partnership, the biggest thing is trust and believing in each other as people, so I think it was really important," Murray said. "As much as I've gotten a chance to talk to him and know him a little bit, to get to know him really well as a person in a scenario where we had no choice but to get to know each other and hang out, it was awesome."

It also served as the starting point for adding some elements of head trajectory to Holtby's game. Minnesota Wild goaltender Devan Dubnyk, who has worked with Mast for the past three summers, offered a demonstration of the technique in a hallway of Capital One Arena when the Wild was in town earlier this month. The key goal is increased efficiency.

"If you think about going from your right to your left and the pass comes, you think being fast is moving and then pushing over," Dubnyk said. That could require four separate actions to accomplish. But, Dubnyk explained, if he moves his head while tracking the puck, "you just stay there, and then, as the puck crosses, if you're watching it and then you just watch it as it gets there, you just push and you're eliminating an

"You've got to keep evolving," Braden Holtby said. (PHOTO BY TONI L. SANDYS)

extra motion."

Basically, it's leading with the head and having the body follow. Holes close more easily because the upper body is always behind the puck and facing the puck, which allows the lower body to come in behind the puck better.

"Imagine if the eyes were stuck in the middle of your sockets," Dubnyk said, "and the only way you'd be able to follow or watch things around would be how you'd look."

Said Holtby: "It's mainly just to give yourself a little more time to react. Some of it makes sense."

That one motion saved could be the split second that differentiates a goal and a save. With a less experienced blue line in front of him this season, Holtby is seeing roughly 4.75 more shots per game compared with last year; this is the first time he has been peppered with more than 30 shots per game since Barry Trotz became coach. But in the company of goalies who have played at least 800 minutes this season, Holtby is fifth in even-strength save percentage (.925) and high-danger save percentage (.842), maintaining his top form even as his teammates have occasionally struggled in front of him.

If a headfirst approach can give Holtby even the slightest edge, he's open to it.

"He's open because he knows how to bring new techniques into his game and new information into his head without being consumed by it," Murray said. "Him learning and trying new concepts is not something that bothers him. It helps him because of the way he internalizes it and manages that information and those techniques and brings it into that whole package that he stays true to."

John
Carlson

FIRST-HALF RESULTS 2017-18

	OPPONENT	RESULT		W-L-OL	GOALIE	TOP PERFORMER	SF-SA	PP	PK
Oct. 5	**at Ottawa**	W	5-4 SO	1-0-0	Holtby	Ovechkin, 3 goals	28-32	0-1	5-5
Oct. 7	**vs. Montreal**	W	6-1	2-0-0	Holtby	Ovechkin, 4 goals	23-39	1-4	4-4
Oct. 9	**at Tampa Bay**	L	4-3 OT	2-0-1	Grubauer	Oshie, 2 goals + assist	26-40	2-4	4-5
Oct. 11	**vs. Pittsburgh**	L	3-2	2-1-1	Holtby	Djoos, goal + assist	22-36	0-4	3-6
Oct. 13	**at New Jersey**	W	5-2	3-1-1	Holtby	Backstrom, goal + 3 ast.	28-23	3-5	3-4
Oct. 14	**at Philadelphia**	L	8-2	3-2-1	Grubauer	Vrana, goal	23-37	0-2	1-2
Oct. 17	**vs. Toronto**	L	2-0	3-3-1	Holtby	Holtby, .966 save pct.	30-30	0-3	2-2
Oct. 20	**at Detroit**	W	4-3 OT	4-3-1	Holtby	Holtby, .919 save pct.	41-37	2-5	4-5
Oct. 21	**vs. Florida**	L	4-1	4-4-1	Grubauer	Smith-Pelly, assist	42-23	0-4	4-6
Oct. 26	**at Vancouver**	L	6-2	4-5-1	Holtby	Stephenson, goal	27-30	0-3	3-6
Oct. 28	**at Edmonton**	W	5-2	5-5-1	Holtby	Ovechkin, 3 assists	31-40	0-0	4-4
Oct. 29	**at Calgary**	L	2-1	5-6-1	Grubauer	Grubauer, .947 save pct.	31-38	0-2	2-2
Nov. 2	**vs. NY Islanders**	W	4-3	6-6-1	Holtby	Eller, 2 goals, assist	19-38	0-4	2-4
Nov. 4	**at Boston**	W	3-2	7-6-1	Holtby	Wilson, 2 goals	27-33	0-2	3-4
Nov. 6	**vs. Arizona**	W	3-2 OT	8-6-1	Holtby	Carlson, goal + assist	40-26	1-6	3-3
Nov. 7	**at Buffalo**	L	3-1	8-7-1	Grubauer	Grubauer, .935 save pct.	25-32	0-1	4-4
Nov. 10	**vs. Pittsburgh**	W	4-1	9-7-1	Holtby	Holtby, .964 save pct.	31-28	2-6	4-4
Nov. 12	**vs. Edmonton**	W	2-1 SO	10-7-1	Holtby	Holtby, .967 save pct.	19-30	0-3	0-0
Nov. 14	**at Nashville**	L	6-3	10-8-1	Holtby	Oshie, 2 goals	29-31	1-3	4-5
Nov. 16	**at Colorado**	L	6-2	10-9-1	Grubauer	Oshie, assist	30-28	1-5	4-6
Nov. 18	**vs. Minnesota**	W	3-1	11-9-1	Holtby	Holtby, .968 save pct.	43-31	2-5	3-4
Nov. 20	**vs. Calgary**	L	4-1	11-10-1	Holtby	Eller, goal	30-39	0-3	3-5
Nov. 22	**vs. Ottawa**	W	5-2	12-10-1	Holtby	Kuznetsov, goal + 2 ast.	25-31	1-1	3-3
Nov. 24	**vs. Tampa Bay**	W	3-1	13-10-1	Grubauer	Grubauer, .962 save pct.	38-26	0-3	2-3
Nov. 25	**at Toronto**	W	4-2	14-10-1	Holtby	Ovechkin, 3 goals	21-29	1-3	1-1
Nov. 30	**vs. Los Angeles**	L	5-2	14-11-1	Holtby	Kuznetsov, 2 goals	29-27	0-2	2-2
Dec. 2	**vs. Columbus**	W	4-3	15-11-1	Holtby	Holtby, .914 save pct.	23-35	1-2	0-0
Dec. 4	**vs. San Jose**	W	4-1	16-11-1	Grubauer	Grubauer, .960 save pct.	29-25	2-6	1-1
Dec. 6	**vs. Chicago**	W	6-2	17-11-1	Holtby	Ovechkin, goal + 3 ast.	25-39	1-3	4-4
Dec. 8	**vs. NY Rangers**	W	4-2	18-11-1	Holtby	Wilson, goal + assist	40-29	0-4	3-3
Dec. 11	**at NY Islanders**	L	3-1	18-12-1	Holtby	Grubauer, 1.000 save pct.	32-29	0-2	3-3
Dec. 12	**vs. Colorado**	W	5-2	19-12-1	Holtby	Kuznetsov, 3 assists	27-24	0-1	4-4
Dec. 14	**at Boston**	W	5-3	20-12-1	Holtby	Chiasson, 2 goals	22-37	1-4	3-5
Dec. 16	**vs. Anaheim**	W	3-2 OT	21-12-1	Holtby	Ovechkin, goal + assist	27-30	0-0	0-1
Dec. 19	**at Dallas**	W	4-3 OT	22-12-1	Holtby	Burakovsky, 2 goals + ast.	28-36	0-3	3-4
Dec. 22	**at Arizona**	L	3-2 OT	22-12-2	Grubauer	Kuznetsov, goal + assist	17-27	0-2	1-2
Dec. 23	**at Vegas**	L	3-0	22-13-2	Holtby	Orlov	26-28	0-4	2-2
Dec. 27	**at NY Rangers**	L	1-0 SO	22-13-3	Grubauer	Grubauer, 1.000 save pct.	30-37	0-2	3-3
Dec. 28	**vs. Boston**	W	4-3 SO	23-13-3	Holtby	Eller, goal + assist	34-34	1-4	5-5
Dec. 30	**vs. New Jersey**	W	5-2	24-13-3	Holtby	Carlson, goal + 2 assists	35-27	1-2	2-2
Jan. 2	**at Carolina**	W	5-4 OT	25-13-3	Holtby	Ovechkin, 2 goals	26-38	0-2	3-4

SECOND-HALF RESULTS 2017-18

	OPPONENT	RESULT		W-L-OL	GOALIE	TOP PERFORMER	SF-SA	PP	PK
Jan. 7	**vs. St. Louis**	W	4-3 OT	26-13-3	Holtby	Backstrom, goal + assist	33-34	2-4	1-2
Jan. 9	**vs. Vancouver**	W	3-1	27-13-3	Grubauer	Grubauer, .974 save pct.	36-38	0-2	2-3
Jan. 11	**vs. Carolina**	L	3-1	27-14-3	Holtby	Holtby, .938 save pct.	28-33	0-3	1-1
Jan. 12	**at Carolina**	W	4-3	28-14-3	Grubauer	Ovechkin, goal + 2 assists	27-39	1-4	3-5
Jan. 18	**at New Jersey**	L	4-3 OT	28-14-4	Holtby	Connolly, 2 goals	19-32	0-5	3-3
Jan. 19	**vs. Montreal**	L	3-2	28-15-4	Grubauer	Carlson, goal	26-26	1-3	3-4
Jan. 21	**vs. Philadelphia**	L	2-1 OT	28-15-5	Holtby	Ovechkin, goal	28-23	1-3	3-3
Jan. 25	**at Florida**	W	4-2	29-15-5	Holtby	Ovechkin, goal + assist	46-34	2-6	4-4
Jan. 31	**vs. Philadelphia**	W	5-3	30-15-5	Holtby	Stephenson, 2 goals	25-30	2-3	1-1
Feb. 2	**at Pittsburgh**	L	7-4	30-16-5	Holtby	Ovechkin, 2 goals + assist	33-39	0-3	1-4
Feb. 4	**vs. Vegas**	L	4-3	30-17-5	Grubauer	Niskanen, goal + assist	23-31	0-2	0-1
Feb. 6	**at Columbus**	W	3-2	31-17-5	Holtby	Holtby, .949 save pct.	25-39	1-1	3-3
Feb. 9	**vs. Columbus**	W	4-2	32-17-5	Holtby	Holtby, .946 save pct.	17-37	1-4	3-3
Feb. 11	**vs. Detroit**	L	5-4 OT	32-17-6	Holtby	Beagle, 2 assists	27-29	2-3	3-3
Feb. 13	**at Winnipeg**	L	4-3 OT	32-17-7	Holtby	Holtby, .909 save pct.	27-44	0-2	3-3
Feb. 15	**at Minnesota**	W	5-2	33-17-7	Grubauer	Ovechkin, goal + 3 assists	27-34	0-2	4-5
Feb. 17	**at Chicago**	L	7-1	33-18-7	Holtby	Wilson, goal	20-44	0-2	3-4
Feb. 19	**at Buffalo**	W	3-2	34-18-7	Grubauer	Grubauer, .941 save pct.	30-34	0-1	3-3
Feb. 20	**vs. Tampa Bay**	L	4-2	34-19-7	Holtby	Ovechkin, goal	37-19	1-2	1-2
Feb. 22	**at Florida**	L	3-2	34-20-7	Holtby	Burakovsky, goal + assist	35-33	1-3	3-4
Feb. 24	**vs. Buffalo**	W	5-1	35-20-7	Grubauer	Kuznetsov, goal + 3 ast.	36-29	1-1	2-2
Feb. 26	**at Columbus**	L	5-1	35-21-7	Holtby	Grubauer, 1.000 save pct.	26-35	1-3	2-4
Feb. 27	**vs. Ottawa**	W	3-2	36-21-7	Grubauer	Kuznetsov, 2 goals	22-30	0-2	6-7
Mar. 3	**vs. Toronto**	W	5-2	37-21-7	Holtby	Backstrom, goal + 2 ast.	34-29	2-2	2-2
Mar. 6	**at Anaheim**	L	4-0	37-22-7	Holtby	Grubauer, 1.000 save pct.	36-18	0-3	0-1
Mar. 8	**at Los Angeles**	L	3-1	37-23-7	Grubauer	Grubauer, .929 save pct.	26-29	0-3	1-1
Mar. 10	**at San Jose**	W	2-0	38-23-7	Grubauer	Grubauer, 1.000 save pct.	26-24	0-0	2-2
Mar. 12	**vs. Winnipeg**	W	3-2 OT	39-23-7	Grubauer	Ovechkin, 2 goals	43-28	1-4	3-3
Mar. 15	**at NY Islanders**	W	7-3	40-23-7	Grubauer	Backstrom, goal + 2 ast.	22-38	1-1	3-3
Mar. 16	**vs. NY Islanders**	W	6-3	41-23-7	Holtby	Chiasson, goal + 2 ast.	31-25	3-8	2-5
Mar. 18	**at Philadelphia**	L	6-3	41-24-7	Grubauer	Carlson, goal + assist	28-35	0-3	3-3
Mar. 20	**vs. Dallas**	W	4-3	42-24-7	Holtby	Ovechkin, goal + 2 ast.	32-27	1-3	3-4
Mar. 22	**at Detroit**	W	1-0	43-24-7	Grubauer	Grubauer, 1.000 save pct.	26-39	0-3	4-4
Mar. 24	**at Montreal**	W	6-4	44-24-7	Grubauer	Backstrom, 4 assists	30-21	2-3	2-3
Mar. 26	**at NY Rangers**	W	4-2	45-24-7	Grubauer	Ovechkin, goal + assist	33-30	1-3	4-4
Mar. 28	**vs. NY Rangers**	W	3-2 OT	46-24-7	Holtby	Holtby, .946 save pct.	33-37	0-3	4-5
Mar. 30	**vs. Carolina**	L	4-1	46-25-7	Holtby	Kempny, goal	21-30	0-2	1-1
Apr. 1	**at Pittsburgh**	W	3-1	47-25-7	Grubauer	Grubauer, .973 save pct.	34-37	0-5	5-5
Apr. 2	**at St. Louis**	W	4-2	48-25-7	Holtby	Holtby, .944 save pct.	34-36	1-2	4-4
Apr. 5	**vs. Nashville**	L	4-3	48-26-7	Grubauer	Kuznetsov, 2 goals + ast.	32-29	2-5	0-2
Apr. 7	**vs. New Jersey**	W	5-3	49-26-7	Holtby	Ovechkin, 2 goals	26-26	0-2	1-1

T.J.
Oshie

THE COACH

BARRY TROTZ

Only one hole to fill on résumé

BY ISABELLE KHURSHUDYAN

In an office decorated with mementos of his long and rewarding career, pictures and keepsakes chronicling the highlights, Barry Trotz allowed himself to dream about an absent image. In his hand, he held a stainless-steel travel mug, engraved to read "2ND FAVORITE CUP."

This wasn't the first time he'd leaned back in his chair and envisioned what he'd do with the Stanley Cup if he ever earned a day with it. "I think that's what motivates you, too," Trotz said last week.

Trotz recently moved into fifth place on the NHL's all-time coaching wins list, 740 to his name in 19 years. His .685 points percentage in three-plus seasons with the Capitals is better than any coach in franchise history. For a third time in his career, he was tabbed as a bench boss for the All-Star Game. He is one of the most respected and accomplished coaches in the league. But just like Washington star captain Alex Ovechkin, Trotz lacks a Stanley Cup on his decorated résumé. He's also never gotten past the second round of the playoffs. If the window to do so is steadily closing for this aging Capitals core, it's especially so for Trotz, 55, coaching on the last year of his contract and potentially in his last opportunity to win with this team.

"I realized I want to have a Cup, but I may not get it as a coach," Trotz said. "It may come as a scout or a GM; it may come in a different form. I don't know. I still want to be a part of a Cup winner. I would like to be the coach, but I wish I could say, 'Yeah, it's going to happen' — and I'm saying that every day to myself, 'It's going to happen, it's going to happen' — but I don't know if it is. And I wouldn't trade anything."

There's a case to be made that this season is Trotz's most impressive coaching job with Washington. The Capitals were discounted after a difficult offseason that saw the departures of forwards Marcus Johansson, Justin Williams and Daniel Winnik and defensemen Nate Schmidt, Karl Alzner and Kevin Shattenkirk. Washington attempted to fill those lineup holes and work around its considerable salary-cap constraints with two rookie blue-liners, two forward prospects and two veteran forwards making the league minimum after their previous teams didn't want them anymore.

The Capitals are somehow in first place in the competitive Metropolitan Division halfway through the season, weathering the roster turnover, early-season injuries and the lingering hurt from last year's disappointing early playoff exit. Since Trotz became coach before the 2014-15 season, the Capitals are first in the NHL in cumulative wins, points, goals and power-play percentage, and they've allowed the fewest goals per game.

"I thought I prepared well, and I'm not even close to what Barry can do," said Dallas Stars Coach Ken Hitchcock, third all-time in wins with 805. "I think the thing that is remarkable about Barry is that nothing is spontaneous. There's a plan for everything. I was surprised how ultra-organized the plan was. ... Barry plans every hour of every day in advance of what he's going to do. There's a reason that his teams are going to be consistent."

Over the course of 15 years, Trotz helped build the Nashville Predators from a lowly expansion franchise to a regular playoff presence through that meticulous attention to detail. "You could beat Nashville, but you could never outwork them," Hitchcock said. But that didn't mean Trotz had no fun. On one occasion, recognizing his team needed to loosen up during a losing streak, Trotz had the Predators' right-handed shooters use left-handed sticks and vice versa, making for a comical practice.

This season required Trotz to similarly relinquish some of the control and order he might prefer. For a second straight year, the Capitals had compiled the league's best regular season record, and for a second straight year, they lost to the Pittsburgh Penguins, eventual Stanley Cup champions. Washington was still in a collective hangover in October, and Trotz knew he needed to give his team some space.

"The teams that have won experienced adversity," said Hall of Fame coach Scotty Bowman, who won 1,244 games and nine championships. "I mean, it's not a good formula, but you usually get pretty close, then you slip down a bit, then you've got to retool or do something different. ... You've just got to keep working at it, that's what I would tell people. You can't drink any kind of Kool-Aid to make it better. You just have to stick with it."

The Capitals floundered through their first 20 games, appearing on the verge of collapse

Barry Trotz moved up to fifth on the NHL's all-time coaching wins list. (PHOTO BY JONATHAN NEWTON)

after November blowout losses at Nashville and Colorado. There was concern that after Trotz's first three seasons all ended with the same result, a heartbreaking second-round loss in the playoffs, players were tuning him out in the fourth year. The time for giving the players space was over, and Trotz was harsh in the locker room after a 6-2 loss to the Avalanche in Denver. It wasn't a guarantee he'd still be the coach at the end of the month, but the Capitals turned a corner the next week, and they're 16-3-2 in the past 21 games.

"We've talked about why certain teams won and why certain teams didn't that we've coached," Hitchcock said. "What were the core ingredients? We spent a long time this summer talking about it. You know, it was a tough summer for him. ... The teams that did have success, they have certain qualities, and we talked about what those qualities were, and how much we could influence those qualities. It was a pretty direct talk, to be honest you. The one thing we came up with, which was really interesting, is you can't be afraid to coach people up."

Working with Ovechkin the past four years has given Trotz a unique perspective on legacies. He doesn't believe Ovechkin's individual accomplishments as the greatest goal scorer of this generation should be tarnished because his teams haven't won a Stanley Cup. Trotz asked if legendary defenseman Ray Bourque had stayed in Boston for his entire career and not won a championship with Colorado in his final game, would he be less of a player? Or what about San Jose center Joe Thornton, who could have more than 1,500 career points but no Cup by the time he retires?

He's talking about others, but he's also talking about himself and how his career will eventually be judged. "I wouldn't trade anything to have a Cup," Trotz said. "I think all the experiences that I've had and what we're doing are the right thing.

"But I want the Cup. There's no question."

Evgeny
Kuznetsov

2017-18 INDIVIDUAL STATISTICS

PLAYERS	GP	G	A	P	+/-	PIM	PPG	SHG	GWG	OTG	S	S%	TOI/G	SFT/G	FO%
Alex Ovechkin	82	49	38	87	3	32	17	0	7	3	355	13.8	20:08	21.1	37.5
Evgeny Kuznetsov	79	27	56	83	3	48	7	1	8	2	187	14.4	18:48	20.3	44.2
Nicklas Backstrom	81	21	50	71	5	46	7	0	4	1	165	12.7	19:39	22.4	51.2
John Carlson	82	15	53	68	0	32	4	0	4	1	237	6.3	24:46	26.4	0.0
T.J. Oshie	74	18	29	47	2	31	9	0	3	0	127	14.2	18:24	20.8	47.9
Lars Eller	81	18	20	38	-6	38	3	0	2	0	161	11.2	15:18	19.0	49.3
Tom Wilson	78	14	21	35	10	187	0	1	1	0	123	11.4	15:59	20.1	46.3
Dmitry Orlov	82	10	21	31	10	22	0	0	2	0	125	8.0	23:07	25.5	0.0
Matt Niskanen	68	7	22	29	24	36	2	0	1	0	120	5.8	22:36	24.9	0.0
Brett Connolly	70	15	12	27	-6	30	4	0	2	0	67	22.4	12:00	15.0	45.2
Jakub Vrana	73	13	14	27	2	12	1	0	2	0	133	9.8	12:29	15.6	52.0
Andre Burakovsky	56	12	13	25	3	27	2	0	5	1	84	14.3	13:50	16.6	54.5
Jay Beagle	79	7	15	22	3	16	0	1	2	0	65	10.8	12:26	18.0	58.5
Alex Chiasson	61	9	9	18	1	26	1	1	2	0	59	15.3	11:45	15.7	26.8
Chandler Stephenson	67	6	12	18	13	8	0	0	0	0	36	16.7	11:52	16.1	54.8
Devante Smith-Pelly	75	7	9	16	-6	38	0	0	1	0	103	6.8	12:20	15.4	48.5
Christian Djoos	63	3	11	14	13	10	0	0	0	0	60	5.0	14:02	18.4	0.0
Madison Bowey	51	0	12	12	-3	24	0	0	0	0	47	0.0	13:42	16.9	0.0
Brooks Orpik	81	0	10	10	-9	68	0	0	0	0	54	0.0	19:21	22.2	0.0
Taylor Chorney	24	1	3	4	8	8	0	0	0	0	14	7.1	12:59	17.5	0.0
Jakub Jerabek	11	1	3	4	-1	0	0	0	0	0	11	9.1	13:59	16.4	0.0
Michal Kempny	22	2	1	3	1	14	0	0	0	0	32	6.3	16:44	19.5	0.0
Nathan Walker	7	1	0	1	1	4	0	0	0	0	4	25.0	9:11	13.0	0.0
Shane Gersich	3	0	1	1	-1	0	0	0	0	0	4	0.0	9:01	12.3	0.0
Travis Boyd	8	0	1	1	2	2	0	0	0	0	2	0.0	8:49	12.5	50.0
Aaron Ness	8	0	1	1	2	8	0	0	0	0	2	0.0	12:43	19.4	0.0
Anthony Peluso	2	0	0	0	0	4	0	0	0	0	0	0.0	4:38	8.0	0.0
Liam O'Brien	3	0	0	0	0	5	0	0	0	0	1	0.0	6:55	10.0	0.0
Tyler Graovac	5	0	0	0	-3	2	0	0	0	0	1	0.0	6:44	10.6	33.3

GOALTENDERS	GP	GS	W	L	OT	SA	GA	GAA	SV	SV%	SO	G	A	PIM	MIN
Braden Holtby	54	54	34	16	4	1,648	153	2.99	1,495	.907	0	0	0	2	3,067:48
Philipp Grubauer	35	28	15	10	3	953	73	2.35	880	.923	3	0	1	0	1,864:48

CAPITALS PLAYOFF HISTORY

	PTS	RK	COACH	W	L	GF	GA	RESULT
1982-83	94	3rd	B. Murray	1	3	11	19	Reached division semifinals
1983-84	101	2nd	B. Murray	4	4	28	25	Reached division finals
1984-85	101	2nd	B. Murray	2	3	12	14	Reached division semifinals
1985-86	107	2nd	B. Murray	5	4	36	24	Reached division finals
1986-87	86	2nd	B. Murray	3	4	19	19	Reached division semifinals
1987-88	85	2nd	B. Murray	7	7	54	50	Reached division finals
1988-89	92	1st	B. Murray	2	4	19	25	Reached division semifinals
1989-90	78	3rd	B. Murray/T. Murray	8	7	49	48	Reached conference finals
1990-91	81	3rd	T. Murray	5	6	29	35	Reached division finals
1991-92	98	2nd	T. Murray	3	4	27	25	Reached division semifinals
1992-93	93	2nd	T. Murray	2	4	22	23	Reached division semifinals
1993-94	88	3rd	T. Murray/Schoenfeld	5	6	32	32	Reached Eastern Conference semifinals
1994-95	52	3rd	Schoenfeld	3	4	26	29	Reached Eastern Conference quarterfinals
1995-96	89	4th	Schoenfeld	2	4	17	21	Reached Eastern Conference quarterfinals
1997-98	92	3rd	Wilson	12	9	53	44	Reached Stanley Cup finals
1999-2000	102	1st	Wilson	1	4	8	17	Reached Eastern Conference quarterfinals
2000-01	96	1st	Wilson	2	4	10	14	Reached Eastern Conference quarterfinals
2002-03	92	2nd	Cassidy	2	4	15	14	Reached Eastern Conference quarterfinals
2007-08	94	1st	Hanlon/Boudreau	3	4	20	23	Reached Eastern Conference quarterfinals
2008-09	108	1st	Boudreau	7	7	41	38	Reached Eastern Conference semifinals
2009-10	121	1st	Boudreau	3	4	22	20	Reached Eastern Conference quarterfinals
2010-11	107	1st	Boudreau	4	5	23	24	Reached Eastern Conference semifinals
2011-12	92	2nd	Boudreau/Hunter	7	7	29	30	Reached Eastern Conference semifinals
2012-13	57	1st	Oates	3	4	12	16	Reached Eastern Conference quarterfinals
2014-15	101	2nd	Trotz	7	7	28	28	Reached Eastern Conference semifinals
2015-16	120	1st	Trotz	6	6	29	22	Reached Eastern Conference semifinals
2016-17	118	1st	Trotz	7	6	36	36	Reached Eastern Conference semifinals
Totals				**116**	**135**	**707**	**715**	**Games played: 251**
2017-18	105	1st	Trotz					Won Stanley Cup finals

Series played: 47. Series won: 20. Division titles: 11.

Nicklas
Backstrom

THE STAR

ALEX OVECHKIN

1,000 games into captain's stellar career, a look back

BY ISABELLE KHURSHUDYAN

Those short drives from Alex Ovechkin's first Washington apartment to the downtown hockey rink were five minutes the Capitals superstar will never forget. A 20-year-old Ovechkin would punch the 601 F St. NW address into his car navigation system, and though he drove there 41 times that season, Ovechkin still needed the directions. Then came the pinch-me moment.

"When I drive to the games, it was an unbelievable feeling, you know?" Ovechkin said. "My dream come true."

Thirteen years after that first Ovechkin season, he's poised to play his 1,000th game with the Capitals on Sunday night in Pittsburgh, the first player in franchise history to reach that milestone. He has evolved from the brazen rookie to the team's captain and longest-tenured player. While the 2005-06 campaign was the dazzling start of one of the most dominant careers in NHL history, this season has seen Ovechkin continue to cement his place in the sport's pantheon, scoring his 600th career goal while leading the NHL with 45 this year.

He still smiles every time he's asked to recall his rookie season. The team's inside joke was that its record was so poor, the Capitals were eliminated in October. But that collection of largely journeymen NHLers raised and influenced a young Ovechkin who needed help navigating sudden stardom.

"Back then, we don't have lots of success as a team, but we have one of the best locker rooms I've ever been in," Ovechkin said. "That group of guys was special almost because the whole group was experiencing it through Alex's eyes," said Jeff Halpern, the captain that season.

Halpern met Ovechkin at the world championships just before the Capitals drafted him first overall in 2004. By then, it was obvious Washington would pick him with the top selection, so Halpern briefly introduced himself.

"I see a kid that I didn't have a huge connection with right away," Halpern admitted.

Then when Ovechkin arrived in Washington a few weeks before training camp, he wore ripped cutoff jean shorts and a too-tight T-shirt to an informal skate. "He looked like a mess," Halpern said, describing it as like the scene from the movie "Slap Shot" in which teammates encountered the outrageous Hanson brothers for the first time.

"We played the Flyers at some point in preseason, and he scored a goal and skated by their bench and winked at their bench," Halpern said. "I was like, 'Oh, this guy is going to get us killed.'"

Nine-hundred ninety-eight games later, Ovechkin's NHL debut stands as the true eye-opener for Capitals players from that season. For all of the hype surrounding him, he had a good-but-not-great training camp. Then on his very first NHL shift, he knocked Columbus's Radoslav Suchy into the glass, shattering it. By the end of the game, he had scored his first two goals. By the end of the season, he would have 52 with 54 assists.

"Our team was not very good, but we made the most of it, and the big reason for that was Ovi," said Matt Bradley, a forward on that team. "I always joked that I had a front-row seat to watch what he did. I mean, he's worth the price of admission on his own, so for me to sit there on the bench and watch him do it was special."

Said Brian Willsie: "We knew he could score, knew he could shoot and had seen that, but just the whole physical game and just the drive every single shift is what we saw that first game, and we hadn't seen that before. We kind of had this stereotypical Russian player who was superskilled but didn't play that physical side. And he did it, and that's what really set him apart and opened all of our eyes."

Ovechkin requested that he have a North American roommate on the road that season to help him adapt to the culture and learn the language, so he was paired with Willsie. "He handle me pretty well," Ovechkin said with a chuckle. Coach Glen Hanlon charged Willsie with being Ovechkin's chaperon and making sure he got to the arena on time after their routine trip to Starbucks. Willsie was endeared by Ovechkin's childlike love for playing, a quality he still has at 32, but he also wanted to teach Ovechkin how to be professional, whether it was getting to bed by a certain time or making sure they had a healthy meal for dinner.

"I got told by Glen Hanlon, 'Just don't lose him,'" Willsie said. "He was like a puppy in those towns — you just don't want to lose him. ...

"Every city we went to was a brand-new experience for him, the first games in every NHL arena. He would grill me with questions in the morning on the way to rink. What's the crowd like? What's the arena like? What's the city like? He was just so excited and curious to play in all of those different cities."

Ovechkin repeatedly wore tight red jeans to practice, "and finally someone said, 'We need to stop with the tight red jeans and take him shopping,'" Willsie said with a laugh. On the team's first trip to New York, Ovechkin asked Willsie to direct him to the fashion strip and go shopping with him. Ovechkin kept trying to buy Willsie some new clothes, but Willsie insisted on just waiting for him by the door.

"It was his first time playing in Toronto, and our regular routine was to go morning skate, come back for lunch and then have a nap and then we'd go back to the game," Willsie said. "This time, we finished our meal and we're getting ready for our nap, and it was around Christmastime in Toronto and he was so excited that we were finally playing Toronto. So, he says, 'I'm going to walk around.' I said, 'Are you sure?' He's like, 'Yep, I can't sleep.' He was gone the whole afternoon. I don't know where he went."

More than anyone, Willsie saw the toll Ovechkin's hulking 6-foot-2, 215-pound body took that first season. "He was pretty beat up that first year," Willsie said. Ovechkin still played all but one game while recording 172 hits, 14th most in the league. Ovechkin's first hat trick came against Anaheim, a game that's remembered as much for his thundering hit on defenseman Vitaly Vishnevski.

"Ovi, he wears those gold chains, and you could hear the chains like a cowbell kind of coming at you," Halpern said.

"The setup that we had in Nashville is we had a big, long hallway, so you could see the visitors down the hall, and when Alex was cutting a stick or something, you realized how huge he is," said Capitals Coach Barry Trotz, then with the Predators. "Big, giant legs. I mean, he's a big man. And I didn't have a real big team, and guys were like, 'Did you see this?' You could hear the conversation. I never saw him off the ice before, and the guys are saying how big he was and then you knew how physical he was. So, we had a couple of nervous cats."

Halpern didn't think the hard-hitting style would be sustainable, comparing it to the short career of an NFL running back. "When you run through enough brick walls, eventually the wall is going to start to hit back," Halpern said. But of players from Ovechkin's 2004 draft class, he's the first to reach 1,000 games, never missing more than 10 in a season. He's been out of the lineup for just 29 games during his career, and 12 of those scratches weren't even injury-related.

"Thanks, God," Ovechkin said while knocking on his wooden locker room stall.

"There isn't a guy who's played a harder 1,000 games than him," Bradley said.

Ovechkin has become more selective with his physicality in the interest of conserving energy, something Trotz asked of him when the two met in Moscow last summer. He has toned down other parts of his game, including the enthusiastic celebrations that initially caught his teammates and the rest of the NHL off guard. The sport prides itself on its players' humility, and though teammates would occasionally tease Ovechkin that first year — "He showed up with blue neon lights underneath his car one day, and we all thought that was pretty funny," Bradley said — they never wanted to destroy his zeal.

It made them look forward to what he might do the next game and the one after that. One thousand games into his career, that wonder and that anticipation remain.

"How do you control a guy like that? How do you tell a guy not to be excited about playing hockey?" Halpern said.

"I was lucky to be drafted here," Ovechkin said. "Right away, I feel this is my second home. The organization, the fans, the community has been great for me. It's nice to play for one team that long time and be able to stay healthy and be able to do all these things together."

Back page: Alex Ovechkin, being recognized for his 1,000th NHL game, said, "I was lucky to be drafted here." (PHOTO BY KATHERINE FREY)

Alex
Ovechkin

ALEX OVECHKIN CAREER STATISTICS

	TEAM	GP	G	A	PTS	PIM	+/-	PPG	SHG	GWG	SHOTS
2005-06	Capitals	81	52	54	106	52	2	21	3	5	*425
2006-07	Capitals	82	46	46	92	52	-19	16	0	8	*392
2007-08	Capitals	82	*65	47	*112	40	28	*22	0	*11	*446
2008-09	Capitals	79	*56	54	110	72	8	19	1	10	*528
2009-10	Capitals	72	50	59	109	89	45	13	0	7	*368
2010-11	Capitals	79	32	53	85	41	24	7	0	*11	*367
2011-12	Capitals	78	38	27	65	26	-8	13	0	3	303
2012-13	Capitals	48	*32	24	56	36	2	*16	0	4	*220
2013-14	Capitals	78	*51	28	79	48	-35	*24	0	10	*386
2014-15	Capitals	81	*53	28	81	58	10	*25	0	*11	*395
2015-16	Capitals	79	*50	21	71	53	21	*19	0	8	*398
2016-17	Capitals	82	33	36	69	50	6	*17	0	7	313
2017-18	Capitals	82	*49	38	87	32	3	17	0	7	*355
Totals		1,003	607	515	1,122	649	87	229	4	102	4,896

*League leader

Hart Trophy (most valuable player): 2008, 2009, 2013

Lester B. Pearson/Ted Lindsay Award (most outstanding player as selected by NHLPA): 2008, 2009, 2010

Art Ross Trophy (top point scorer): 2008

Maurice "Rocket" Richard Trophy (top goal scorer): 2008, 2009, 2013, 2014, 2015, 2016, 2018

Calder Memorial Trophy (rookie of the year): 2006

NHL first all-star team (2006, 2007, 2008, 2009, 2010, 2013, 2015)

NHL second all-star team (2011, 2013, 2014, 2016)

NHL All-Star Game (2007, 2008, 2009, 2011, 2012, 2015, 2016, 2017, 2018)

NHL all-rookie team (2006)

WASHINGTON
capitals
C
8
CCM